Bible Class for Youth and Adults: Beginner's Guide: Deuteronomy

BIBLE CLASS FROM SCRATCH, Volume 5

Bible Sermons

Published by Guillermo Doris McBride, 2024.

BIBLE CLASS FOR YOUTH AND ADULTS: BEGINNER'S GUIDE: DEUTERONOMY

First edition. October 20, 2024.

Copyright © 2024 Bible Sermons.

ISBN: 979-8227914262

Written by Bible Sermons.

Table of Contents

Dedication

Deuteronomy 6:1. Now these are the commandments, statutes, and judgments, which the LORD thy God commanded to teach thee, that thou shouldest do them in the land whither thou goest to possess it: That thou mayest fear the LORD thy God, to keep all his statutes and his commandments which I command thee, thou, and thy son, and thy son's son, all the days of thy life; and that thy days may be prolonged.

Obedience to God must arise from fear of Him, or from a holy fear of God felt in the heart, for all true religion must be the work of the heart. It is not the mere action that God looks at, but the motive, the spirit that dictates it. Therefore it is always said, "That thou mayest fear the Lord thy God, that thou mayest keep all his statutes and commandments." Nor should we be content to keep the commandments ourselves. It is the duty of parents to see to the good of their children, to see to it that the child and the child's child walk all their lives in the ways of God. May God grant that we may never be partakers of the spirit of those who think that they have no need to care for the religion of their children, who seem to leave it to a blind fate. May we care for them with this care so that our child and our child's child may walk before the Lord all the days of his life.

Deuteronomy 6:3. Hear therefore, O Israel, and observe to do it, that it may go well with thee, and that thou mayest multiply, as the LORD God of thy fathers hath promised thee, in a land flowing with milk and honey.

It seems, according to the old covenant, that temporal prosperity was added as a blessing to the observance of God's commandments. It has sometimes been said that while prosperity was the blessing of the old covenant, adversity is the blessing of the new, and there is some truth in that statement, for whom Jehovah loves he chastens, and yet it is true that it is best for a food to walk in the commandments of God. There is a sense in which we make the best of both worlds when we seek the love of God. When we seek first the Kingdom of God and his righteousness, other things are added to us; so that it is not without significance for us that the Lord here promises temporal blessings to his people.

— **Charles Spurgeon**

Introduction

———

A s we come to the book of Deuteronomy, we must remind you that this is the last book of the Pentateuch. The first five books of the Bible were written by Moses and constitute the Pentateuch. These books are the following: Genesis, Exodus, Leviticus, Numbers, and Deuteronomy.

A book full of valuable teachings and promises from God to his people. In Deuteronomy, we will find important instructions and exhortations that will guide us in our walk as followers of Christ.

In this book, we will see how Moses recapitulates the commandments and laws that God had given to the people of Israel, reminding them of the importance of obeying and trusting the Lord at all times. Through Moses' words, we will learn about God's faithfulness, His unfailing love and His desire for His people to live in holiness and obedience.

During our upcoming meetings, we will explore together the truths and lessons that Deuteronomy holds for us, and how we can apply them to our daily lives. May this study inspire us to live with integrity, to love God with our whole being, and to follow His ways with faithfulness and devotion. Get ready for a journey of spiritual growth and strengthening of our faith! Let's begin this exciting journey together in the book of Deuteronomy! Accompanied by God's grace and wisdom, we are ready to dive into His Word! Welcome everyone!

Titles

T he word Deuteronomy, the name given to this book in the Greek translation of the Old Testament, means the second law. We are not to infer that it was a repetition of the law as given to Moses on Mount Sinai. This was more than a recapitulation. It was another example of the law of repetition or recurrence, which we have seen before in the Holy Scriptures. The Spirit of God has His method of saying something in the form of an outline or general plan, and then returning to it and emphasizing a particular portion of what He has said. It is the method God used to call our attention to certain matters of special importance. Specific laws that needed emphasis were repeated and dealt with in detail. For example, this was the case for the Ten Commandments in chapter 5.

There are four Hebrew titles of Deuteronomy.

1. Debarim - "The Words" or "These are the Words", which is derived from the first sentence of the book.

"These are the words which Moses spoke to all Israel on this side Jordan" (Deut. 1:1). These words that Moses spoke can be classified into an outline, the main divisions of which would be as follows:

I. The first 4 chapters look back on the journeys of the children of Israel. Moses reviewed their history for this new generation.

II. He then reiterated the law in chapters 5 to 26: in this section we find a repetition and interpretation of the 10 commandments (chapters 5 to 7), a series of religious and national rules (chapters 8 to 21) and a series of rules for domestic and personal relationships (chapters 22 to 26) Then, having looked back into the past, we come to another section,

III. in which he looked ahead, into the future, and the author presented one of the greatest prophetic portions in all of Scripture (in chapters 27 to 30). Finally, there is a requiem to Moses in chapters 31 to 34. Thus, this entire outline comes from one of the names of the book of Deuteronomy - "Debarim" or "The Words". Continuing with the other Hebrew titles of this book we have:

2. The Kith or Fifth Book of the Law.

3. The Book of Reproaches, and

4. Reiteration of the Law.

The writer

Moses wrote Deuteronomy. Moses was a man who knew God, and with whom God spoke face to face. The children of Israel saw the works of God, but they did not know Him. Moses did know His purposes. *"His ways he declared unto Moses, and his works unto the children of Israel,"* Psalm 103:7 tells us. Deuteronomy was the result of this intimate knowledge, in addition to the experience of the 40 years in the wilderness.

The section dealing with the death of Moses, Deuteronomy 34:5-12, was probably written by Joshua and belongs to the book of Joshua. When this book of Joshua was written, it was placed in the Pentateuch scroll, making it a Hexateuch.

The book of Deuteronomy has been the focus of attack by critics. The literary paternity of the book was first questioned. The original criticism was that Moses could not have written it because the art of writing did not exist in Moses' time. That criticism was later refuted absolutely, since it is now known that writing existed long before the time of Moses.

Then the critics declared that the purpose of the book was to glorify the priesthood in Jerusalem, but neither the priesthood nor Jerusalem are mentioned in Deuteronomy.

Much of this criticism was derived from the Graf-Wellhausen hypothesis, which emerged many years ago from German universities. It is still taught in many of the seminaries in the United States.

The probable reason for the satanic attack against the book of Deuteronomy is that the Lord Jesus Christ quoted exclusively from this book when Satan tempted him.

The first temptation - (Matthew 4: 4 and Luke 4: 4) In that passage, Satan suggested to Jesus to turn stones into bread. Jesus quoted Deut. 8:3, and said: Man shall not live by bread alone, but by every word that proceeds from the mouth of God.

The second temptation - (Matthew 4: 7 and Luke 4:12) In this passage, Satan offered Jesus to throw himself from the pinnacle of the temple. Then Jesus quoted from Deut. 6:16, and said: Thou shalt not tempt the Lord thy God.

The third temptation - (Matt. 4:10 and Luke 4: 8) In this passage, Satan took him to a place from which he showed him and offered him all the kingdoms of the world. Then Jesus quoted from Deut. 6:13 and 10:20; and said, Thou shalt worship the Lord thy God, and him only shalt thou serve.

Deuteronomy exalts the Word of God. "And these words which I command you today shall be upon your heart" (Deut. 6:7). It is not the Bible you carry under your arm, or the one you keep in your library as a souvenir, that is important. Rather, it is the Bible that you open before your eyes and that you study and read. The Old Testament prophets quoted frequently from Deuteronomy. In the New Testament there are more than 80 references to the book.

The Topic

The theme of this book is love and obedience. Some may be surprised that the theme of God's love is mentioned so early in Biblical history. The word "love" appears 22 times, and "obey" appears 10 times.

The motive for obedience is love. The Lord Jesus was not trying to teach something new. He was teaching an eternal truth, when He said, in John 14:15, "If ye love me, keep my commandments". This book teaches that obedience is a response to God's love. The true motive for obedience is stated in Deut. 6:4,5: "Hear, O Israel: the Lord our God, THE Lord is one. And thou shalt love the Lord thy God with all thy heart, and with all thy soul, and with all thy might".

Man's love for God is the motive of his obedience. This is not the gospel, but its great principle is found here. This will help us to have a fair view of the law. Let us understand one thing. The law is good!

Although we emphasize the fact that we cannot be saved by the law, this does not imply that the Law is not good. Of course, the law is good! So where is the problem? The difficulty is with you and with each one of us. Consequently, God has to save us only by His grace.

The principle of love and obedience is the path of blessing. It is also the answer to those who do not find love in the Old Testament. Love is found in the Old Testament, just as the law is found in the New Testament. Moses pleaded with the people to obey. They had to obey because Israel belonged to God. God loved them and wanted to keep them and prosper them. They were to show God their gratitude.

God has given us laws because He loves us. His laws are eternal, and great blessing results from obeying those laws. The difficulty lies in the human heart.

The purpose of the book

The book of Deuteronomy was written for that new generation that had arrived on the east bank of the Jordan River (Deut. 1:5), which was not familiar with the experiences of Mount Sinai. They had arrived on the east bank of the Jordan River, and they had one month left to enter the Promised Land (Deut. 1:3). The adults of the generation that had left Egypt were already dead and their bones were disintegrating under the desert skies because of their unbelief and disobedience. They had violated the law of God by the sins they had committed. They had demonstrated their lack of faith in God, which encompassed their sins of omission, that is, those things they should have done and did not do. For unbelief is sin!

As we said before, it is not that the law was bad, but that it was incapable of being put into practice because of human weakness. The Apostle Paul said in Romans 8:3, *For God has done what the law of Moses could not do, which it was unable to do because of human weakness.* God sent His Son in the very weakness of sinful man and as a sacrifice for sin, thus condemning sin in the very weakness of our condition. The flesh was evil as it is today. That was the reason why God had to have a totally different basis for saving us.

This new generation of adults needed to receive the law interpreted in the light of thirty-eight years of wilderness experience. New problems not specifically addressed by the law had arisen. As an example of new situations, let us recall, from our study of the book of Numbers, that the daughters of Zelophehad had come before Moses and told him that their father had no living male children. The family consisted of those five women. The law said that a male child was to inherit the land, and so they asked him if they would have the right of inheritance, or if the land would cease to be their father's family's if they could not inherit it. Therefore, there had to be an interpretation of the law, and the interpretation was that women, those who were heirs, could inherit the land just like men.

On the other hand, God also told His people that they should constantly teach the Law to their children. By the way, I wonder if this is not a neglected area in the home of our time and in some sectors of contemporary Christianity.

Moses gave this new generation the Lord's final instructions before yielding, at his death, the leadership of the nation. He reviewed the wilderness experiences, and emphasized again certain aspects of the law. He made known to them their next journey, in the light of the Palestinian covenant, which God had made concerning the Promised Land. In this book we will not only see that the Mosaic law was not only given to a people, but that it was also given to a land. Finally, Moses taught them a new song, blessed the twelve tribes, and prepared to die. The book concludes with a requiem to Moses.

To recapitulate, Deuteronomy follows the form or outline of the treaties that the kings of the second millennium B.C. concluded with a vassal country, which leads us to fix an early date for the writing of this book. But in spite of the aforementioned outline, the nature of this work is rather of the sermon type. Moses was preaching the law to the Israelite people, so that the Word of God would be engraved in their hearts. His goal was to get the people to renew the covenant made at Mount Sinai. In other words, his purpose was to achieve a renewed commitment to the Lord. For only by committing unconditionally to the Lord could those people enter, conquer and take possession of the Promised Land, to live in peace and prosperity. Let us now consider,

Deuteronomy 1:1-3

S ubject: the failure of Cades-Barnea

It is important to note here that the first four chapters of this book give a retrospective look at the journeys of the children of Israel. In fact, these four chapters constitute the first speech that was delivered by Moses. This speech extends from Deut. 1:6 to Deut. 4:40. Moses is recalling his past history and, specifically, the journeys of the Israelites and interpreting many of the events that occurred. All of that generation had died, with the exception of Caleb and Joshua. He was preparing the new generation to enter the Promised Land, and reviewing the experiences of their fathers, so that the new generation would profit from them and not repeat the failures of their forefathers. Let us read verse 1 of this first chapter of Deuteronomy:

"These are the words which Moses spoke to all Israel on this side Jordan, in the wilderness, in the Arabah, opposite the Red Sea, between Paran, Tophel, Laban, Hazeroth, and Dizahab."

From that mountain, it is possible to see the city of Jerusalem. What is seen today does not appear to be, in any way, a promised land. It looks more like an uninhabited land, and this reveals what has happened to that land over the centuries. When Moses looked at it from the top of that mountain, we believe he saw a flourishing and good land. Today, it is a desert. Let us continue reading verse 2:

"Eleven days are from Horeb, on the way to the mountains of Seir, to Kadesh-barnea."

Mount Sinai is in Horeb. It was a journey of about eleven days from Horeb to Kadesh-barnea. This was the entrance to the Promised Land.

Israel spent 38 years wandering, when it should have taken only eleven days to enter the land. Why? Because of their unbelief. Their march became a wandering wandering, and they became simply strangers and pilgrims in that wilderness. This is the sad result. Why was it so? Because they were slow to learn. They went astray because of their unbelief and wandered for thirty-eight years in that vast and terrible wilderness.

We too are late learners, dear listener. We think we would describe ourselves by saying that we have a low mental quotient, spiritually speaking. Let us continue reading verse 3, of this chapter 1 of Deuteronomy:

> *"And it came to pass in the fortieth year, on the first day of the eleventh month, that Moses spake unto the children of Israel according to all that the Lord had commanded him concerning them."*

At the end of their time of wandering in the wilderness, Moses delivered his first speech to them. Obviously, His words were first given verbally, and then later they were written down. Moses was the spokesman who delivered the speech, and yet he made it clear that these words were revealed to him by the Lord.

The theme of this book is based on love and obedience, as well as the purpose of its author to instill in those people the spiritual and human values of the divine Revelation, both in the relationship between human beings and God, as well as in the horizontal relationship of the social coexistence of people. This theme is highly relevant to the times in which we live. Obedience to divine laws seems to human beings to be impossible to comply with or, in the best of cases, they are considered a heavy burden to bear. It is because these laws are opposed to sin and the control it maintains over human nature. But when the human heart is captivated by the love of God revealed in Jesus Christ and in his work of salvation on the cross, the feelings of redeemed human beings, freed from slavery, feel gratitude towards God. And the more they come to love him, the more gratifying it is for them to live according to the will, words and principles of their Creator and Savior. And I think we all understand that situation, with which, on a human level, we are so familiar. Have we not felt a real satisfaction in pleasing those we love? So it is with those who love God.

Deuteronomy 1:9-2:5

―――

We continue today studying Deuteronomy chapter 1. And in our previous episode, we talked about how Moses was reminding the Israelites of their wilderness wanderings. And we were saying that Mount Sinai is in Horeb. And that from Horeb to Kadesh-barnea, which was the entrance to the Promised Land, was a journey of about 11 days. Now, Israel spent 38 years wandering in the wilderness when they should have traveled only 11 days to enter the Promised Land. And all because of their unbelief.

Now, at the end of that time of pilgrimage, Moses delivered his first speech. His words were expressed verbally, but later they were written down. Moses was the spokesman who gave the speech. However, he made it clear that these words had been revealed to him by the Lord Himself. Let us continue today to consider,

The failure of Cades-Barnea

In recalling in detail his history and his journeys, Moses mentioned his first mistake. Let us read verses 9, 12 and 13 of this chapter 1 of Deuteronomy:

"At that time I spoke to you and said to you, 'I alone cannot bear you..... How shall I alone bear your troubles, your burdens, and your strife? Give me from among you, from your tribes, wise and understanding and expert men, that I may appoint them as your leaders."

We find the account of this incident in Exodus chapter 18. Moses became irritated, feeling very frustrated. He believed that he alone was bearing the burden of Israel. Then the Lord allowed him to appoint elders, and so a committee of 70 elders was formed. This committee would eventually become the Sanhedrin, the organization that many years later would deliver Jesus Christ to death.

Moses, in his frustration, lost sight of the fact that it was God who was bearing with Israel. Moses was God's appointed leader and needed no Board or Committee. He made a mistake on that occasion, and it was a mistake that several generations later would lead to the crucifixion of Christ. And Moses made mention here of that mistake. Very few people would point out his failures, but Moses acknowledged them. He said that at first it had seemed to him a very good measure, but it did not work out and caused many difficulties.

Now, do you want to know Moses' assessment of the wilderness through which they passed? Let's read verse 19:

"When we departed from Horeb, we went through all that great and terrible wilderness which you saw, by the way of the mountain of the Amorites, as the Lord our God commanded us, and we came to Kadesh-barnea."

And we will have to take his word for it, because he was there. It was a vast and inhospitable desert. The journey of the children of Israel through the wilderness did not consist precisely in following a flowery path.

The second mistake Moses recorded was the decision made at Kadesh-barnea. This was a mistake of the people. And once again, it was the result of having a deliberative group or committee. Let us continue reading verses 20 to 23:

"Then said I unto you, Ye are come unto the mountain of the Amorites, which the Lord our God giveth us. See, the Lord, your God, has given you the land: go up and take possession of it, as the

Lord, the God of your fathers, has said to you. Fear not, nor be dismayed. But you all came near and said to me, "Let us send men ahead of us, and let them search the land, and when they return, let them bring us an account of the way by which we are to go up and of the cities we are to come to. The proposal seemed good to me, and I took twelve men from among you, one man from each tribe.

Here we see that they considered it necessary to have a coordinating group to go in and explore the land. God had already recognized it! God had said it was a land rich in agriculture and livestock. Of course there were giants in the land, but God had said that He would take care of them. The people wanted to have that group of observers and Moses agreed. And we know what happened. This was the reason why they returned to that terrible desert.

The fundamental problem was their unbelief. God had said it was a good land. And the spies went through it and agreed that it was a good land. They said there were giants in the land. But God had said that He would deal with the giants because He would enable Israel to deal with that situation. But, they did not believe God.

The Christian is often confronted by giants in his life. We are sure that as a child of God you have also found yourself, figuratively speaking, in the land of giants, that is, facing people or seemingly insurmountable difficulties. Believe us, it is difficult to know how to deal with a giant when you feel like a pygmy yourself. God has given us the same promise. He can take care of the giants, those gigantic circumstances, for us. And it's wonderful to know that. It's not usually the external factors that are our real problem. It's our internal circumstance that causes the problems.

Now, God told them plainly that all the generation that came to Kadesh-barnea, and that fell back in unbelief, would die. A whole new generation had arisen. God was now speaking to this new generation through Moses. This new generation was to take advantage of those experiences of their fathers. They were to learn from them for their own entrance into the Promised Land. There were only two men left from the old generation, two men who were allowed to enter the Promised Land and they were Joshua and Caleb. Let us turn now to verse 34 and read through verse 38 of this Deuteronomy chapter 1:

"When the LORD heard the voice of your words, he was angry and swore this oath, Not one man of this evil generation shall see the good land which I swore to give to your fathers, except Caleb the son of Jephunneh; he shall see it, and I will give to him and to his sons the land which he trod, because he has faithfully followed the LORD. The LORD was also angry with me for your sakes, and said unto me, Thou shalt not go in thither. Joshua the son of Nun, who serves you, he shall go in thither; encourage him, for he shall give it to Israel."

Caleb and Joshua were very different from the others. They were among the spies who believed God and brought back an accurate report, a good report. The fact is that Caleb succeeded in taking possession of the land he wanted to have. We will see later in the book of Joshua that he was an extraordinary man. He went through that land and claimed precisely the mountain where the giants lived! And when the time came, he said to Moses: *Give me now this mountain. And God gave it to him and to his descendants.*

By the way, what do you want from God? Are you a father or mother? Are you a young person who is beginning to struggle in this life? What do you want from God? Let us say this: Perhaps by now you have discovered that you cannot just sit and watch, and then pretend to get what you want. For it is not simply a matter of praying, and praying, and praying. Of course we agree that we must pray, and that it is necessary to maintain a relationship of fellowship with God. But it is clear that we must go out and fight to take possession of what we desire. Let us remember that God said He would give Caleb the land on which he had set his foot. Many of us today, we do not receive blessing because, figuratively speaking, we spend too much time sitting. That's not where we should be. We need to walk, to get moving. Much is said in the Scriptures about the Christian's walking, but very little is said about the Christian's sitting. We must take possession of what God has promised us!

Joshua was the man who was to become the leader to succeed Moses. Why was he chosen? He was a man of experience and also faithfully followed God. He had been the other spy who brought back a good report along with Caleb, at the completion of the reconnaissance of the land. In other words, these two men believed God. That was the bottom line. They believed God and were willing to step out in faith. you don't believe God by simply sitting in a passive wait-and-see attitude and demanding the great blessings. We must step out by faith to get involved in God's cause. Let us continue reading verse 39:

"And your children, of whom you said they would serve as a spoil, and your children, who know neither good nor evil today, they shall go in thither; to them will I give it, and they shall inherit it."

There are some very important things here that we do not want to overlook. In the first place, the age at which people attain responsibility is older than we think it is. Some of these who entered the Promised Land were between the age of thirteen and nineteen in Kadesh-barnea. We know from our study of Numbers 14:29 that God set the age at 20, and all those over 20 died in the wilderness.

God did not hold responsible those young men who had not reached the age of responsibility, when the elders of the people refused to enter the Promised Land, but allowed them to enter the land. It was because those of the old generation had said that they did not want to enter the land because they were thinking of the safety of their children;

and God expressed very clearly that this was not their true motive. They were insulting God. They were really saying that God would not take care of the children. Then God said to them, *"Yes, I care for your children; and those little ones whom you thought were in great danger are precisely the ones who will enter the land."* And that generation of young people had reached the border of the land and were ready to enter the Promised Land. And it was to them that Moses addressed himself. Let us now read verses 40 and 41 of this chapter 1 of Deuteronomy:

"But you turn and go into the wilderness, on the way to the Red Sea. Then you answered and said to me: We have sinned against the Lord. We will go up and fight, according to all that the Lord our God has commanded us. And you armed yourselves every man with your weapons of war and prepared to go up to the mountain.

After the children of Israel had refused to enter the land at Kadesh-barnea, they faced a tremendous dilemma. They had sinned against God. They faced the wilderness if they turned back, that wilderness which Moses had referred to as that great and terrible wilderness. Recognizing then that they had sinned, and realizing what they faced in the wilderness if they turned back, they declared that they would enter the land after all. Let us read verse 42 of this Deuteronomy chapter 1:

"But the Lord said unto me, Say unto them, Go not up, neither fight, for I am not among you; lest ye be overthrown by your enemies."

Let us tell you that such fighting was not good. And do you know why? Because they were outside the will of God. The reason they were willing to fight this time was not because they believed God, but because they were afraid. Their motivation was fear, not faith. They were driven by fear, and not by faith in God. Now, verse 43 tells us:

"I spoke to you, but you did not listen to me; rather you were rebellious against the command of the Lord, and by persisting haughtily you went up on the mountain."

Here it was not about faith. If they had gone up in the beginning because they believed God, it would have been different. But this attitude reveals that they acted presumptuously and that was a totally different situation. We believe there is a clear distinction between faith and presumption.

Let us now continue reading verses 44 to 46 of this chapter 1 of Deuteronomy:

"But the Amorites that dwelt in that mountain met you, and chased you as the wasps do, and defeated you in Seir until you came to Hormah. Then you returned and wept before the LORD, but the LORD did not listen to your voice or pay attention to you. Therefore you had to stay in Kadesh all the time that you were there".

Notice this, dear listener. They came before the Lord and shed crocodile tears. They wept and repented. Yes, but what kind of repentance was this? Listen to what the apostle Paul told us in his second letter to the Corinthians 7:10, *The sorrow that is according to God worketh repentance to salvation, whereof there is no repentance; but the sorrow of the world worketh death.*

But let us return to our passage. Were they weeping because they had disobeyed God? No. They wept because the Amorites had persecuted them. Defeat was the reason for their weeping. You know that when an offender is arrested, he begins to weep, he sheds tears and repents. But what kind of tears are those? Is he crying because he is a thief? No. He cries because he has been arrested. There is a big difference between genuine repentance and regret for being caught. And that is exactly what we see here with the Israelites. And as a consequence of all this, they spent a long time in Kadesh-barnea.

And so we conclude our study of Deuteronomy chapter 1. And we come now to,

Deuteronomy 2:1-5

———

Topic: Days in the desert

This speech of Moses continued with the review of their journeys. After they turned back at Kadesh-barnea, the children of Israel headed toward Mount Seir, and as verse 1 of chapter 2 says: for a long time we went around the mountains of Seir. We have always thought that the Lord has a sense of humor, and we believe it was evident in this phrase, in which Moses continued speaking, in verses 2 and 3:

"Then the Lord said to me, 'It is enough for you to have compassed this mountain; turn you northward.'"

It is also evident that they did not know where to go. All they had been doing was going around Mount Seir, until at last God told them that He was getting tired of it.

And we fear that many Christians do the same. Because they fail to take God's Word seriously. They are stalling, not moving forward, and getting stuck. There are lessons here in this Deuteronomy chapter 2 that we need to learn. Let us now continue reading verses 4 and 5 of this Deuteronomy chapter 2:

"Say to the people, 'When you pass through the territory of your brethren, the sons of Esau, who dwell in Seir, they will be afraid of you; but you be very careful. Do not meddle with them, for I will not give you of their land even that which covers the sole of a foot, for I have given the mountains of Seir as an inheritance to Esau."

There is something else here that is important for us to learn. In Genesis chapter 36 we learned that Esau lived in Seir and that Esau was Edom.

Jacob, as the eldest son, had received the birthright, and he received from God the promise that his descendants would have the promised land. Esau went to Seir, and it was evident that God had given that part to Esau's people as a possession. Today this land is in Jordan, the country where Petra, the rock-hewn city preserved to this day, is located. God then clearly told the Israelites that they could not touch Esau's possession.

Now, here is a lesson also for the nations. God has fixed the boundaries of the nations, as the apostle Paul said in the book of the Acts of the Apostles 17:26, speaking to the Athenians: From one blood he has made all the seed of men to dwell on all the face of the earth; and he has fixed for them the order of the times, and the bounds of their habitation. Many wars have broken out because the boundaries of nations have not been respected.

Another lesson we must learn is that God always keeps His promises. Even to a people like Esau's people, God remained faithful to what He had promised.

And we say goodbye today, reaffirming our confidence in the veracity of God's promises and inviting you to share this faith, which we find confirmed in the Apocalypse, the last book of the Bible, in which He is seated on the throne and says: Behold, I make all things new. And the divine voice said to the author of this book: Write, for these words are faithful and true.

Deuteronomy 2:7-4:12

———

Today we continue studying Deuteronomy chapter 2. And in our previous episode, we talked about "God's care for His people in the wilderness". And we saw in verses 4 and 5 of this chapter 2, how God told the Israelites clearly, that they could not touch Esau's possession. In Genesis, chapter 36, we learned that Esau lived in Seir and that Esau was Edom. Jacob had received the birthright and received the promise that his descendants would have the promised land. Esau, on the other hand, went to Seir and it was clear that God had given that part to Esau's people as a possession. Now, there is a lesson here also for the nations today. God has prefixed the boundaries of the nations, as the apostle Paul says, back in the book of the Acts of the Apostles, chapter 17, verse 26, speaking to the Athenians, and he says to them, *"And of one blood hath he made all the seed of men, that they should dwell on all the face of the earth: and he hath appointed unto them the order of times, and the bounds of their habitation."* Many wars have broken out because the boundaries of nations have not been respected.

Another lesson we must learn is that God always keeps His promises. Even to a people such as Esau's people. God remains faithful to His Word. Let us now continue with verse 7 of this Deuteronomy chapter 2:

"For the Lord, your God, has blessed you in all the works of your hands; he knows that you are wandering in this great wilderness, and during these forty years the Lord, your God, has been with you, and you have lacked nothing."

We have here an overview that encompassed all those forty years. God knew all their trials and difficulties. Yet Moses could truly say, "and you have lacked nothing." It was the same case with David who, when he reflected on his life, was able to say in Psalm 23:1 "The Lord is my shepherd; I shall not want." How was it possible for him to say this because he had never lacked anything! God does not promise us the luxuries of life, but God provides for the necessities of life. And he will do that with you and also with me, dear listener. And let's move on to consider now,

God's care for other nations

We have already seen how God protected Esau's boundaries. And we see that he did the same with the other nations. Let's read verse 9 of this Deuteronomy chapter 2. Moses said:

"Then the Lord said to me, 'Do not trouble Moab or make war against him, for I will not give you possession of his land, for I have given Ar as an inheritance to the sons of Lot.'"

Turning now to verse 19, where we read:

"And when you come near the children of Ammon, do not trouble them or quarrel with them, for I will not give you possession of the land of the children of Ammon, for I have given it to the children of Lot as an inheritance."

The children of Israel would face giants in the land, but God encouraged them by showing them that in order to conquer their land, Esau also had to destroy the giants called Horites, as we see here in verse 22, where it says:

"as the Lord did to the children of Esau that dwelt in Seir, before whom he wiped out the Horites; they evicted them and dwelled in their place to this day."

And the children of Ammon in order to possess their land, they also had to conquer the giants, which they called "Zomzomites" as we see here in verse 20, where it says:

"It was also considered a land of giants; giants once lived there, whom the Ammonites called Zomzomites.

Apparently there were whole nations of giants in those lands. Let's see now,

The conquest of Transjordan

L et us read verse 24 of this chapter 2 of Deuteronomy:

"Arise, go forth, and pass over the brook Arnon. I have delivered into your hand Sihon king of Heshbon, the Amorite, and his land. Begin to take possession of it and go to war with him."

The Israelites surrounded the lands of Moab and Ammon. However, God told them not to take possession of their land. These nations sold them food and drink. But God told them that when they asked Sihon the Amorite to allow them to do the same, he would not let them pass. Therefore, they were not to be afraid to fight and conquer him.

God would allow Israel to conquer and possess the land that had previously belonged to the Moabites. The Amorites, under the leadership of Sihon, had expelled the Moabites from this area and conquered their territory. God had allowed him to dispossess the Moabites, but when that king directed his attack against Israel, he was killed and his forces were scattered. His capital city fell and the territory was given to Israel. This episode would often be mentioned as a reminder to Israel of what God had done for them and became a source of encouragement. God was showing them that He was with them and that He would be faithful to His promises.

God allows us to go through certain experiences. Sometimes he sends us through difficult experiences, or sad ones, to prepare us for life. Or perhaps God uses them to prepare us so that we can help others in their trials. And so we conclude our study of Deuteronomy chapter 2. And we come to,

Deuteronomy 3

Theme: The defeat of Og, king of Bashan (the conquest and possession of the land east of the Jordan).

We will quickly go through this chapter, because it is not our intention to go into detail about this journey through the wilderness. All this is still part of Moses' first speech, in which he recalls the experiences of his journeys. Journeys that we have already seen in our study in the book of Numbers. Now Israel fought with Sihon the Amorite, and took all his cities and destroyed the people. They took the cattle, and the spoil of the cities. We are told this at the end of chapter 2. Let us begin, then, by reading the first two verses of this chapter 3 of Deuteronomy. Moses said:

"So we returned and went up on the way to Bashan. Then Og king of Bashan came out to meet us with all his people to fight at Edrei. But the Lord said to me, 'Do not be afraid of him, for I have delivered him into your hand, along with all his people and his land. You shall do to him as you did to Sihon, the Amorite king of Heshbon.

Here, we will not go into details, because this is a repetition of the information we already had in our study of chapters 21 to 25 of Numbers. Let us now look at the paragraph referring to,

Possession of the promised land

Let us read verses 12 and 13 of this chapter 3 of Deuteronomy:

"This land which we inherited at that time, from Aroer, which is by the brook Arnon, even unto the midst of the mountains of Gilead with the cities thereof, I gave to the Reubenites and the Gadites. The

rest of Gilead and all Bashan, of the kingdom of Og: all the land of Argob, which was called the land of the giants, I gave to the half tribe of Manasseh."

This is a review of the fact that the two and a half tribes chose to stay on the east side of the Jordan, receiving the kingdom conquered from Og. They agreed to send to the west side of the Jordan an army of men to help the other tribes fight their battles. Their wives, children, and cattle, remained on the eastern side. We have already studied this incident in Numbers 32. Let us turn to the last paragraph of this chapter, entitled,

The prayer of Moses

Here Moses recalled his personal experience with the Lord and why he would not be allowed to enter with the people into the Promised Land. Let us read verses 23 to 26:

"At that time I prayed to the LORD, and said, O Lord GOD, thou hast begun to shew thy servant thy greatness and thy mighty hand: for what god is there in heaven or on earth that doeth such works and such mighty acts as thine? Let me pass over, I pray thee, and see that good land beyond Jordan, that goodly mountain, and Lebanon. But the LORD was angry with me because of you, so he would not listen to me, but said to me, "It is enough; speak no more to me about this matter.

Like a good father, God was faithful to His Word. It's as if He said to him, "That's enough. I don't want to hear any more about this matter!" Let's continue reading verse 27:

"Go up to the top of Pisgah and lift up your eyes to the west, the north, the south, and the east, and see with your own eyes, for you will not pass over the Jordan."

Our heart sympathizes with Moses when he pleaded with God to allow him to enter the land that had been his goal for forty years. What a great lesson we have here! Even if we repent of our sin, we have to bear the consequences of it in this life, whether we like it or not. And God told him in verse 28:

"Train Joshua, encourage him and strengthen him, for he is to pass over before this people, and he will give them the land which you shall see."

Moses was making it clear to this generation that was ready to enter the Promised Land, that Joshua was the man the Lord had chosen to be their leader. And so we come to,

Deuteronomy 4:1-12

———

S ubject: an admonition to the new generation.

We are coming to the conclusion of Moses' first speech. He had reviewed his travels. Moses and the people were then on the east bank of the Jordan River. They had reached Mount Nebo, and Moses was giving them his final instructions. As he spoke to them, he looked back on that entire journey. Only two men who were there had made the entire journey with Moses. They were Joshua and Caleb. Most of the people had been buried in the wilderness. All the rest were members of the new generation and were ready to enter the land, but first Moses had wanted to review the experiences of the wilderness. We now come to the paragraph entitled,

Moses pleaded with them to obey God

L et us read the first two verses of this chapter 4 of Deuteronomy:

"Now therefore, O Israel, hear the statutes and judgments which I teach you, that ye may do them, and live, and go in and possess the land which the Lord, the God of your fathers, giveth you. Ye shall not add unto the word which I command you, neither shall ye diminish from it, that ye may keep the commandments of the Lord, your God, which I command you."

They were to fulfill the Word of God. They were not only to hear it, but to make it a reality in their lives. They were not to add to the law, nor were they to take anything away from it. They were to fulfill it as God had given it.

If Israel had kept the law, what a blessing it would have been! But, we see here a demonstration in history of a people who received the law in favorable circumstances, but could not obey it. Let us remember the statement that no human being will be justified before God by the law. Why? Because God is arbitrary? No. It is because human nature is radically evil. That is the problem.

We have already indicated that this book emphasizes two great themes: love and obedience. Perhaps you never realized that love was a big theme of the Old Testament, but it was. Here, in this fourth chapter of Deuteronomy, Moses pleaded with this new generation to obey God, and gave the reasons why they should obey Him.

1. First, God wanted to preserve and prosper Israel. This first verse tells us that they were to obey the Lord and listen to His statutes and decrees "that - as the Lord said - you may live, and go in and possess the land". Obedience to God was the only basis on which He could bless them. He desired their obedience because it was His desire to bless them.

2. Secondly, Israel's obedience would show their thankfulness to God. Let us read verses 5 to 8, of this chapter 4:

"Behold, I have taught you statutes and judgments, as the Lord my God commanded me, that ye should do so in the midst of the land which ye are about to enter to possess it. Keep them therefore, and do them, for they are your wisdom and your understanding in the sight of the people, who shall hear all these statutes, and say: Surely a wise and understanding people, this is a great nation. For what great nation is there that has gods so near to them as is the Lord our God in all that we ask of him? And what great nation is there that hath statutes and righteous judgments such as all this Law is, which I set before you this day?"

God had blessed them in such a wonderful way that they were to show their gratitude through obedience.

3. Now, thirdly, the love of God was to impel them to obedience. Let us go on to verse 37:

> *"Because he loved your fathers, and chose their seed after them, and brought you out of Egypt by his presence and by his great power."*

This was the first time in the Bible that God told anyone that He loved them. God had shown that He loved mankind from the beginning of Genesis. But until that time He had said nothing about it, and this was the first time He spoke of His love for anyone. He declared that this love had been the reason for all that He had done. He had delivered them from the land of Egypt, and He would do even greater and mightier things for them. The basis of it all, the motive, was that God loved them.

This is something that every person today should recognize. No matter who you are, God loves you! You may not always feel God's love. Our sins are obstacles between God and us. But in spite of our sin, God loves you and me. He has demonstrated that love in the cross of Christ. When we receive Christ as Savior, we can experience God's love.

4. Fourth, they were to obey God because they belonged to him. Verse 1 of Deuteronomy, chapter 14, says: "You are sons of the Lord your God; you shall not cut yourselves or shave your heads for the sake of a dead man".

Obedience to God is the first law of life, dear listener. Man has a natural and innate hatred of God. Man does not want to obey God. In fact, man is very much opposed to God. Throughout the Word of God we find that there is a resistance on the part of man against God. We find that in every person even today.

Let us tell you, if the Word of God does not break human resistance, nothing else will. Only God can do it. If Israel had only obeyed God's law, what a blessing they would have had! Let us go back to the beginning of this Deuteronomy chapter 4 and read verses 3 and 4, to see,

Results of obedience and disobedience

"Your eyes saw what the Lord did on account of Baal-peor: every man who followed Baal-peor the Lord, your God, exterminated from among you. But you who followed the Lord, your God, are all alive today."

He was referring to the time when Balaam was called to curse Israel, but was unable to do so. The fact is that it was only possible for him to pronounce blessings. But he made a suggestion to King Moab. He advised the king that, since he could not curse the people, the king should let his people initiate relations with the Israelites so that intermarriage could take place with them. This would implant false worship among them and, consequently, God would judge them. And this is exactly what happened. You will recall that we saw this in Numbers chapter 25. This should serve as an example to this generation, and it should also serve as an example to us.

There was a reward for their obedience. Those who did follow the Lord would retain life and enter the land. God reminded them again that obedience brings with it blessing. Let us continue with verse 5:

"Behold, I have taught you statutes and ordinances, as the Lord my God commanded me, that ye should do so in the midst of the land which ye are about to enter to take possession of it."

Obedience would bring God's blessing. They would enter the land to take possession of it. And their obedience was to serve yet another end. Let us read verse 6:

"Keep them therefore, and do them, for they are your wisdom and your understanding in the sight of the people, who shall hear all these statutes, and say: Surely a wise and understanding people, a great nation is this."

Israel was to be a witness to the whole world. It was to witness to the world in a way that was the opposite of the way the church witnesses to the world. We, as a church, are commanded by God to go into all the world to preach the gospel. That command is given to every believer. Every believer in Christ should have some part in the task of proclaiming the Word of God to the ends of the earth.

Now, frankly, the Israelites were never commanded to go out as missionaries. They were to invite, as the words "Come, we will go to the house of the Lord" expressed. Their obedience, their loyalty to God, would cause the other nations to hear these statutes, and they would take notice that God's blessings would make Israel a great nation. And then what would they do, what did, for example, the queen of Sheba do? Well, she came from the ends of the earth. She made a long and arduous journey. Now, if a woman came and traveled all that distance under such circumstances, don't you think some men would also come to see as well? And they came. So in that way, Israel testified to the world. If they obeyed him, God would bless them and it would serve as a testimony to all nations. But, if they did not obey him and turned away from the Lord, then God would send judgment upon them. Let us now read verse 9:

"Therefore take heed to thyself, and keep thy soul diligently, lest thou forget the things which thine eyes have seen, and lest they depart

from thy heart all the days of thy life; but shalt teach them thy children and thy children's children."

God gave the nation of Israel the great task of a teaching ministry. They were to obey God and they were to teach these things to their children and grandchildren.

The greatest responsibility of any nation is the education of its youth. Probably the greatest failure of any nation is also the lack of such education. Now, we are not blaming the universities or the schools. Do you know where the problem lies? It is precisely at home. God told the Israelites to instruct their children and grandchildren. This was the great responsibility that God placed upon every father and mother in Israel.

if you bring a child into this world, you are responsible for that child. Our problem today is not international relations or the economy. Our problem is the home. God will hold the parents of broken homes responsible for those children left to their own devices, who never knew the teaching, the love, the interest, the communication of their parents. What a great responsibility this is! God made it very clear to Israel. When the nation failed, it was because it had failed at home. And God judged her for it.

Let us now see that this is also a chapter with great spiritual richness. Let us turn to verse 12 of this chapter 4 of Deuteronomy:

"Then the Lord spoke to you out of the midst of the fire; you heard the voice of his words, but except for hearing the voice, you saw no figure."

The Lord Jesus clearly stated the following. You will remember the words of John 4:24: "God is a Spirit; and they that worship him must worship him in spirit and in truth". They were not to have any figure of God in any way. The Lord Jesus became a man, but the Bible did not give us any physical description of Him. But although no one can imagine what He looked like, nor can you see Him in His real appearance, you can have the experience of feeling Him in your heart. You need to accept by faith what He did on the cross by dying in your place. Jesus can be your Savior and Lord today. Then yes, with the eyes of faith, you will be able to feel His presence in a real and definitive way.

Deuteronomy 4:24-5:21

―――

We continue today to consider the results of obedience and disobedience in the nation of Israel, here in this Deuteronomy chapter 4. And we will begin by reading verses 24 through 27:

"For the Lord your God is a consuming fire, a jealous God. When you have begotten children and grandchildren, and have grown old in the land, if you corrupt yourselves and make any graven image or likeness of anything, and do evil in the sight of the Lord, your God, to provoke him to anger, I testify this day to heaven and earth that you will soon disappear completely from the land which you are about to take possession of at the passage of the Jordan. You will not be in it long days without being destroyed. The Lord will scatter you among the peoples, and you will be left only a few among the nations to whom the Lord will lead you."

That nation is, even today, a testimony to the world, although a testimony of their disobedience. Today, they are scattered all over the world. Why? Because they did what God forbade them to do. But someone will say that they are back on earth, and that they are now a nation. Yes, but they have serious problems, don't they? When God brings them back to the land, as He has foretold, they will not have the difficulties they have today. The nation of Israel is still under God's judgment, because they have turned their back on God. And judgment will come upon any nation that rejects God. Let us now read verses 30 and 31 of this Deuteronomy chapter 4:

"When you are in distress and all these things overtake you, if in the last days you turn to the Lord, your God, and obey His voice, for the

Lord, your God, is a merciful God: He will not leave you nor destroy you nor forget the covenant which He swore to your fathers."

This was the first mention of the great tribulation that will come at the end. The phrase "in the last days" is a technical term in the Old Testament and refers to the great tribulation period. Now, God set a condition: "In those last days" that is, in the great tribulation, if they turn to God and are obedient to His voice, He will fulfill the covenant He made with their forefathers and will not forsake them or destroy them. Verse 31 says:

"For the Lord your God is a merciful God: he will not fail you, nor destroy you, nor forget the covenant which he swore to your fathers."

Now, let us observe this: Does God do this because he is cruel? No. God is merciful and for that reason the Israelites have not been consumed.

It is for that very reason that you and I have not been consumed. If you are saved, it is not because you have been kind and gracious. It is because of God's mercy that you are saved. He is merciful to us, just as He has been to Israel.

Moses continued to show them the evidence of God's great mercy toward them. Let us continue reading verses 33 and 34:

"Have any people heard the voice of God speaking out of the midst of the fire, as thou hast heard it, without perishing? Or hath God sought to come and take unto himself a nation out of the midst of another nation, with trials, and with signs, and with miracles, and with war, and with a mighty hand, and with an outstretched arm, and with fearful deeds, as all that the Lord your God did unto you in Egypt before your eyes?"

God did all these things in the sight of his parents. Now, God did not want them to forget about it. God had been very kind to them and wanted them to remember it. Let's turn now to verse 37:

"Because he loved your fathers, and chose their seed after them, and brought you out of Egypt by his presence and by his great power."

God did it because he loved them. That was the explanation. There was no good in them. Instead, there was a lot of goodness in God.

God loves us today. But he does not save us by love. He saves us by grace. He could not simply open the back door of heaven, to let us sneak in. He could not be just and yet act that way. A sacrifice had to be made for our sins. God's love sent Christ to die for us, and Christ loved us enough to die so that you and I could have forgiveness. "For God so loved the world that he gave his only begotten Son, - he did that - that whosoever - no matter who he is - whosoever believeth in him should not perish, but have everlasting life." Now, verses 44 and 45, present the, conclusion and summarize well the content of this chapter 4. They say:

"This then is the law which Moses set before the children of Israel. These are the testimonies, the statutes, and the judgments which Moses commanded the children of Israel when they came out of Egypt."

And so we conclude our study of Deuteronomy chapter 4.

Deuteronomy 5:1-21

T heme: the repetition of the Ten Commandments.

This was Moses' second discourse. It consisted of a reiteration of the law and the emphasis continued to be on love and obedience. In chapters 5 to 7 we will find a repetition and interpretation of the Ten Commandments. The generation that had heard the law in the beginning, back on Mount Sinai, had already died. This new generation, the Israelites who were to enter the land, needed to have the law repeated to them, and also to have it interpreted for them. Moses interpreted it in the light of 40 years of experience in the wilderness.

Some will say that this was a duplication of Exodus chapter 20. Well, it was almost a duplication. It shows that the Ten Commandments were important enough to repeat. They are fundamental moral laws. So let us begin by reading the first verse of this Deuteronomy chapter 5, which begins the paragraph entitled,

The repetition of the ten commandments

H ere you have the four important steps that we must take into account in relation to the Word of God. The first is to hear it. The second is to learn it, to know what God is saying. The third is to keep it. That means to have it engraved in the heart. Let us remember how David spoke of this reality. He said in Psalm 119:11, *"Thy words have I hid in my heart, that I might not sin against thee."* The fourth step is to execute it. Not only must it be in the head and in the heart, but also the Word of God must reach where the feet and hands are, transforming itself into action.

Let us tell you that there are many who say that they live according to the Ten Commandments and that these constitute their religion. It is important to examine such people to find out what they believe. You will discover that what they really mean is that they agree with them. They have heard them and believe them to be good, but they certainly do not obey them.

In reality the law is like a plumb line, which determines the verticality of a crooked wall. It is like a mirror placed in front of the heart. It is like the headlight of a car that illuminates the road in the darkness and reveals the curves ahead.

God made it very clear that He does not save men by keeping a moral code. There is nothing wrong with a moral code. But there is something radically wrong with us. The apostle Paul stated this in his letter to the Galatians 2:16, he said, "Knowing that a man is not justified by the works of the law, but by the faith of Jesus Christ, even we have believed in Jesus Christ, that we might be justified by the faith of Christ, and not by the works of the law: for by the works of the law shall no flesh be justified." No one is justified by the law. Why not? Because no one can do the works of the law.

Then, what is the purpose of the law? asked the apostle Paul, in the same letter to the Galatians 3:19. And he answered: "It was given afterward, to make manifest the disobedience of men, until that seed should come to whom the promise was made. The law was proclaimed by angels, and Moses acted as intermediary. It is logical to ask what is the purpose of the law. The answer is that it was added because of transgressions, until the time when the seed should come. That is, it was temporary until the seed should come, which was Christ. And the apostle Paul added in verses 24 and 25 of the same letter to the Galatians, and also in chapter 3: "The law, like the slave who watches over the children, accompanied us until the coming of Christ, so that through faith we might attain to righteousness. But now that faith has come, we are no longer under the care of that slave which was the law. The law, then, served as a tutor, like that slave who led the child by the hand, to bring us to the cross, just as that slave led the child to school. The law therefore brings us to the cross and says: "You are a sinner and you need a Savior". The purpose of the law, then, is to reveal to us our need of a Savior. The law is good, dear hearer; there is no doubt about it. The law reveals the mind of God. It reveals how far you and I are from the glory of God. The law reveals that "...all have sinned, and are far from the glorious presence of God". So let this law bring you to Christ. Turning now to Deuteronomy chapter 5 that we are studying, let us read verses 2 and 3:

"The Lord our God made a covenant with us in Horeb. Not with our fathers did the Lord make this covenant, but with us, all of us who are here today alive."

God did not give the law to the patriarchs. He did not give it to the Israelites when they were there in Egypt. The law was not given to them until they were in the wilderness, in Horeb, on Mount Sinai. The law was given to the nation of Israel. Let's continue with verses 4 through 7:

"The Lord spoke face to face with you on the mountain out of the midst of the fire. Then I stood between the Lord and you to speak to you the word of the Lord, because you were afraid of the fire and did not go up to the mountain. He said, "I am the Lord your God, who brought you out of the land of Egypt, out of the house of bondage. You shall have no other gods before me".

It is that when the Israelites lived in Egypt, they were surrounded by idolatry. Now, man's first sin was not that of becoming an atheist. His sin was to become a polytheist, that is, to worship many gods. For example, at the tower of Babel they built a "ziggurat", that is, a tower.

At the top of the tower they offered sacrifices, apparently dedicated to the sun. It seems that the sun and the planets were among the first objects that humans worshipped when they turned away from God. After the flood, they undoubtedly did not worship thunder and lightning because they feared them. But they worshipped the sun, that is to say, they dedicated their worship to the creatures before the Creator. Therefore, it was to the polytheist that God said: "Thou shalt have no other gods before me". It was not until the time of David that atheism was introduced. Before that time, human beings were too close to the origin of revelation to be atheists. The revelation of God was still in their memory and no one denied the existence of God. In his time, David said in Psalm 14:1: *"The fool says in his heart, There is no God."* The word "fool" means lacking in reason. A man who says there is no God is either unreasonable, or insincere. This first commandment did not even mention unbelief in the existence of God. The commandment said that they should not worship many gods. Let us continue reading verses 8 to 10 of this chapter 5 of Deuteronomy:

"Thou shalt not make unto thee any graven image, or any likeness of any thing that is in heaven above, or that is in the earth beneath, or that is in the water under the earth. Thou shalt not bow down thyself unto them, nor serve them: for I am the Lord thy God, the mighty, the jealous God, visiting the iniquity of the fathers upon the children unto the third and fourth generation of them that hate me, and shewing mercy unto thousands, unto them that love me and keep my commandments."

There are only two kinds of people in the world: those who hate God and those who love Him. Now, he went into detail about forbidding the making of images of anything that could be worshipped. Later God said, "And thou shalt love the Lord thy God with all thy heart, and with all thy soul, and with all thy might." The Lord Jesus said this was the great commandment. In contrast to this option is the great number of people who hate God even today.

Many say today that they do not worship any idol at all. But the apostle Paul told us in his letter to the Ephesians 5:5 that greed is idolatry. Anything to which one gives oneself completely, anything that comes between us and God, becomes our idol. You will say that you have no idol. But anyone or anything that occupies the first place in your heart, standing between God and you, becomes your idol. Let us now read verse 11:

> *"You shall not take the name of the Lord your God in vain, for the Lord will not hold him guiltless who takes his name in vain."*

Let us remember that when the apostle Paul taught us that all mankind is sinful, he wrote the following in his letter to the Romans 3:14: "Their mouth is full of cursing and bitterness". All one has to do is walk down the street today, or find himself in any public place, and then he will hear how foul-mouthed people express themselves. God abhors that kind of talk, and He abhors those filthy thoughts of the heart that, in that way, come out. God says that He will not hold innocent the one who misuses His name.

The first three commandments were negative. But now we come to a positive commandment. Let us read verses 12 through 15 of this chapter 5 of Deuteronomy:

> *"You shall keep the Sabbath day to keep it holy, as the Lord your God has commanded you. Six days you shall labor and do all your work, but the seventh day is a sabbath of rest to the Lord your God. Thou shalt not do any work, thou, nor thy son, nor thy daughter, nor thy manservant, nor thy maidservant, nor thine ox, nor thine ass, nor any beast of thine, nor the stranger that is within thy gates, that thy manservant and thy maidservant may rest as thou didst. Remember*

that thou wast a servant in the land of Egypt, and that the Lord thy God brought thee out thence with a mighty hand and with an outstretched arm: therefore the Lord thy God hath commanded thee to keep the sabbath."

The most interesting thing here is that all the commandments are repeated in the New Testament, with the exception of the commandment concerning the Sabbath. That commandment was not given to the Church. The Church has always met on the first day of the week, the day on which Christ rose from the dead. The Sabbath has a peculiar relationship with the nation of Israel. In the book of Exodus 31:13, God said: "Thou shalt speak unto the children of Israel, and say unto them, Verily ye shall keep my sabbaths: for it is a sign between me and you throughout your generations, that ye may know that I am the Lord that sanctify you, that I have chosen you". This day was given as a special sign to Israel.

It is interesting to note that in Exodus chapter 20, the Israelites were commanded to keep the Sabbath, because in six days God had created the heavens and the earth. Here in Deuteronomy the Sabbath demonstrated the peculiar relationship between God and the Israelites. And why did the Israelite have to keep the Sabbath? Because he had been a slave in Egypt and God had delivered him by His great power.

These commandments have dealt with duties to God. We now come to the section that establishes the duty to one's neighbor. Let us read verse 16:

"Honor thy father and thy mother, as the Lord thy God hath commanded thee, that thy days may be long, and that it may go well with thee upon the land which the Lord thy God giveth thee."

We believe that this commandment is related to the duty to God and man. The father and mother represent God to the child in the years of his physical development. The child respects the father and mother, and that is as it should be. Proverbs 5:18 tells us: "Listen, my son, to the instruction of your father, and do not forsake the instruction of your mother". The father and mother represent God when the child is young.

Now, upon entering the land that God had promised them, these people were to honor their fathers and mothers. a nation that does not fulfill this commandment will not be blessed. And this is a major problem today. Although we realize perfectly well that not all fathers and mothers are worthy of this respect. God has something to say to them as well. The apostle Paul writing in his letter to the Ephesians 6:4 said: "And you fathers, do not provoke your children to wrath, but bring them up in the discipline and admonition of the Lord". Both commandments should be considered together. Let us now read verse 17 of this Deuteronomy chapter 5:

"Thou shalt not kill."

The word for "kill" here is a very technical word and is "ratsach" and means "to murder". This is personal. This word contains the idea of murder or killing with premeditation, the idea of anger, and personal grievance. This has nothing to do with war. We will read later that God commanded the Israelites to destroy their enemy in the Promised Land. This commandment does not apply to a soldier under orders received during a war. Let us continue now in this Deuteronomy chapter 5 and read verse 18:

"Thou shalt not commit adultery."

We live in a time when human beings like to boast of sexual freedom. Any nuance to any limitation to this alleged freedom is considered an intolerant stance. This is evident in advertising and in the media. God's commandment is still valid today. This type of sin degrades human dignity, social coexistence and the institution of the family. We could say that they constitute another form of slavery. Let us now read verse 19:

> *"Thou shalt not steal."*

It is true that there are many who can say that they have never stolen by snatching other people's things. However, there may be the desire to steal in the heart, and there may be other less obvious ways of stealing, even by omission, in the face of non-compliance with certain laws. Our Lord taught that the very thoughts of the heart are sinful. Hatred in the heart makes one guilty of murder. Just as lust in the heart makes one guilty of adultery. Let us continue with verses 20 and 21:

> *"Thou shalt not bear false witness against thy neighbor. Thou shalt not covet thy neighbor's wife, nor desire thy neighbor's house, nor his land, nor his manservant, nor his maidservant, nor his ox, nor his ass, nor any thing that is thy neighbor's."*

The commandment against covetousness teaches that it is a sin simply to desire excessively something that belongs to another person.

These prohibitions are based on a perfect knowledge of our human nature. And this can only be transformed by God, when a person, recognizing his condition, and that he cannot attain salvation by himself, allows himself to be reached by the grace of God revealed in Jesus Christ. have you experienced that regeneration?

Deuteronomy 5:27-6:25

———

W e continue to consider the second speech of Moses. The generation that had heard the original reading of the law at Mount Sinai had died. In this speech, Moses reiterated and interpreted the law to this new generation that was ready to enter the Promised Land, in the light of their forty years of experience in the wilderness. As we read in verses 27 to 29, the heads of the tribes and the elders said to Moses:

"Come near, you, and hear all that the Lord our God says. Thou shalt tell us all that the Lord our God shall say unto thee, and we will hear and obey. The Lord heard your words when you spoke to me, and said to me, I have heard the words of this people, what they have said to you; all that they have said is well; would that they always had such a heart, that they might fear me and keep all my commandments all the days, that it might be well with them and with their children forever!"

The problem was that the nation had promised to obey the law but failed. The Israelites would be under favorable conditions when they lived in the promised land. The law had been given for that land and for those people. But, it was not possible for them to keep the law, and that should serve as a lesson for us. Just as it was not possible for them to keep it, it is not possible for us to obey it.

The law is a mirror held up before us and will reveal to each of us that we are sinners. The stains are seen. The physical mirror reveals that the face is dirty, but the mirror will not make the stains disappear. The law can reveal our sin, but it cannot save us. We need to use water to wash ourselves and remove the dirty spots. The law is the mirror that tells you to start washing, dear listener. It tells us to come to Christ. It is the blood of Jesus Christ, the Son of God, that will wash us and will continue to wash us from all sin. There is a song that expresses this truth eloquently and it says, "There is a precious spring of Emmanuel's blood, which purifies everyone who dips into it."

In truth, the important thing is not whether you approve of the Ten Commandments, or not, or what you think about them. The important thing is whether you have obeyed them. If you are sincere, you will know that you have not lived up to those principles. That means you need a Savior. Said the prophet Isaiah in 1:18, *"Come quickly, saith the Lord, and let us reason together: though your sins be as scarlet, they shall be as white as snow; though they be red like crimson, they shall be as wool".* When you come to Christ, He will forgive you and cleanse you from all unrighteousness. Then you will be blameless before Him.

Thus, we arrive at,

Deuteronomy 6 and 7

———

Theme: To love and obey

We are sure that you have noticed that in the book of Deuteronomy there has been a special emphasis placed on two words: love and obedience.

The love of God is really expressed in the law. The great principle of the Law is love. Consequently, the principle of the Gospel itself is expressed in Deuteronomy. Which is also expressed in John 3:16, which says: *God so loved the world, that he gave his only Son....*

You and I express our love for God in our obedience. The Lord Jesus put it this way: "If you love me, keep my commandments" (John 14:15). That is still the litmus test today. If we love Him, we will keep His commandments. Salvation is a matter of love. "We love Him, because He first loved us" (1 John 4:19).

The Lord Jesus cited this commandment as the most important of all: "And thou shalt love the Lord thy God with all thy heart, and with all thy soul, and with all thy might" (Deuteronomy 6:5). In this chapter and throughout the book, the emphasis is on keeping the commandments. For obedience is the evidence of love.

We could ask ourselves what is new about love in the New Testament, if love is found in the Old Testament. The difference is that in the New Testament, God's love has been expressed in history, through the incarnation and death of Christ. "But God commendeth his love toward us, in that, while we were yet sinners, Christ died for us" (Romans 5:8). He died for us! It is one thing to express love by leading the Israelites out of Egypt; it is another thing to die for them! It is one thing to say something from the summit of Mount Sinai; it is another thing to descend and assume our weak humanity, becoming like men; and to die on a cross for our sins. We repeat: salvation is a relationship of love. As 1 John 4:10 says, *"Herein is love, not that we loved God, but that He loved us, and sent His Son to be the propitiation for our sins".*

We are still studying Moses' second discourse. In chapters 5 through 7, he presented a repetition and interpretation of the Ten Commandments. Let us now read verses 1 and 2 of Deuteronomy chapter 6, which begin the paragraph entitled,

The great commandment

"These then are the commandments, statutes, and judgments which the Lord your God commanded to teach you, that you may do them in the land to which you are going over to possess it, that you may fear the Lord your God, keeping all the statutes and commandments which I command you, you, your son, and your son's son, all the days of your life, that your days may be prolonged."

The emphasis is on obedience. In reality, there are only two kinds of people in the world: those who love God and those who do not. The heart attitude of people is evidenced by their obedience, or by their disobedience. Listen to the words of Deuteronomy 5:29 "O that they had such an heart, that they would fear me, and keep all my commandments all the days of all my commandments, that it might be well with them and with their children for ever!" Through the prophet Isaiah 29:13, God said the following, *"Therefore saith the Lord, Because this people draw near unto me with their mouth, and with their lips do honor me, but their heart is far from me, and their fear of me is but a commandment of men which they have been taught."* Remember how the prophet Samuel rebuked King Saul, *"Surely to obey is better than sacrifice, and to heed than the fat of rams"* (1 Samuel 15:22). When the

Lord Jesus entrusted His mission to Simon Peter, He asked him a single question, *"Simon, son of Jonah, do you love Me?"* (John 21:16).

The most wonderful thing in heaven will be to see the Lord Jesus and fully realize that He loves us and gave Himself for each one of us. But wonderful also will be that you will love everyone, and everyone will love you. That will make heaven a wonderful place. Let us now read verse 3 of this 6th chapter of Deuteronomy.

"Hear therefore, O Israel, and take heed to do them, that it may go well with you in the land flowing with milk and honey, and that you may multiply, as the Lord, the God of your fathers, has spoken to you."

They had promised to obey all the Lord's commandments, yet they failed. The same thing is happening to us today.

Now, we come to a statement considered by many theologians to be one of the greatest statements in the entire Bible. Let us read verse 4:

Hear, O Israel: the Lord our God, the Lord is one.

"The Lord" corresponds to the Hebrew word formed by the four letters YHWH or JHVH, translated as Jehovah. God is the translation of Elohim, which is a plural word. Since no number is given with it, one may think that the number is three. In Hebrew, a name is singular, dual or plural. When it is plural but no number is given, one can deduce that it refers to the number three. Therefore, this is a reference to the Trinity and could be translated "Hear, O Israel: the Lord our Elohim (the Trinity), the Lord is one".

Israel lived in a world of idolatry. The nations were polytheistic; that is, they worshipped many gods. The message that the nation had to transmit to the world was the message of the unity of the Godhead.

The Lord our Elohim, One is. That is the message for a world given to idolatry.

Today we live in a world characterized not so much by idolatry and polytheism, but by atheism. In today's world, we must communicate the message of the Trinity. There is the Father, the Son, and the Holy Spirit. We are talking about the Lord Himself. He is our Elohim, our Trinity. But He is One. He goes on to say verse 5;

> ***"You shall love the Lord your God with all your heart and with all your soul and with all your strength."***

As we said before, our Lord cited this as the chief commandment of all. In Mark 12:28-31, it says, "And one of the scribes came to him, who had heard them reasoning, and knew that he had answered them well, and asked him, Which is the first commandment of all? Jesus answered him, The first commandment of all is, Hear, O Israel; the Lord our God, the Lord is one. And thou shalt love the Lord thy God with all thy heart, and with all thy soul, and with all thy mind, and with all thy strength. This is the first commandment. And the second is like unto it, Thou shalt love thy neighbor as thyself. There is no other commandment greater than these".

Do you obey this commandment, and is it not true that we all need to confess today that we do not put it into practice? We do not love Him with all our heart and soul. Would that we could keep it. But we need to say like the apostle Paul in Philippians 3:13,14, "Brethren, I myself do not claim to have already attained it; but one thing I do: forgetting those things which are behind, and reaching forward to those things which are ahead, I press toward the goal for the prize of the high calling of God in Christ Jesus."

Yes, we want to say today that we love Him. We wish we loved Him more, but He is the object of our affection. We can truly say that we love Him. That is what He asked Simon Peter. "Do you love me?" We believe that today, He asks the same question of each of us, and He asks it of you too.

To learn to love Him we must sit at His feet and know Him better. As we read in John 6:68, 69, we should say with Peter, "Lord, to whom shall we go? You have the words of eternal life. And we have believed and know that you are the Christ, the Son of the living God." He is our Savior. He is our Lord. He is our God.

Continuing with the incident in Mark 12 where the scribe questioned Jesus, after Jesus quoted to him the words "And thou shalt love the Lord thy God with all thy heart, and with all thy soul, and with all thy might" the Lord Jesus went on to answer him and quoted from Leviticus 19:18, "...thou shalt love thy neighbor as thyself", and said that the latter was similar to the former. there is no such thing as loving God and hating His people. Do you remember that early in the history of the church Saul was persecuting Christians, and the Lord Jesus appeared to him and asked him, "Saul, Saul, why do you persecute me?" (Acts 9:4) Let us tell him that we must be careful in saying that we love Him, when we are showing our contempt for some believers.

Let's go back to our Deuteronomy chapter 6 and read verse 6:

"These words which I command you today shall be upon your heart."

You will recall that, in Psalm 119:11, David said, "Thy word have I hid in mine heart, that I might not sin against thee". That is where you and each one of us should keep the Word of God, dear listener. It should be in our hearts. Let's continue reading verses 7 through 9:

"Thou shalt repeat them unto thy children, and shalt talk unto them, when thou sittest in thine house, and when thou walkest by the way, when thou liest down, and when thou risest up. Thou shalt bind them as a sign upon thy hand, and they shall be as frontlets between

thine eyes; thou shalt write them upon the doorposts of thy house and upon thy gates."

Paul said the same thing in Ephesians 6:4: *"And you, fathers, do not provoke your children to wrath, but bring them up in the discipline and admonition of the Lord".* God has given parents the responsibility to bring up their children in the discipline and instruction of the Lord. Throughout the Scriptures much is said concerning the responsibility of parents. Proverbs 22:6 says: *"Train up a child in the way he should go, and when he is old he will not depart from it.* This does not mean to train him in the way you want him to go. It means that God has a way for him to follow, and that you must cooperate with God's purpose. It means, Father, that you must stay close to God.

These words are to be kept before them at all times. You know how profusely certain products are advertised today, by all means and within the reach of people's sight. God instructed them that His Word should be constantly present and visible among them. And He wants the same for us today. Why? Because He knows that the human heart is prone to forget His Word and His Will. That is how God wants His Word to be taught to His people. It must be considered in all circumstances of life. This is very important.

Then, God admonished His people telling them that they should not forget Him after they entered the land and experienced His blessings. It is strange but, when people are blessed, they tend to forget the One who has blessed them. Let us continue reading verse 13 of this Deuteronomy chapter 6.

"The Lord thy God shalt thou fear, him only shalt thou serve, and by his name shalt thou swear."

Our Lord Jesus used this verse when He was tempted by Satan. We find that he mentioned this quote in Matthew 4:10 and Luke 4:8. And verse 16 says:

"You shall not tempt the Lord, your God, as you tempted him at Massah."

This is another verse our Lord used when resisting Satan's temptation. He quoted it in Matthew 4:7 and Luke 4:12. No wonder Satan hates the book of Deuteronomy so much and launches his attacks against it! Let us continue reading verses 23 to 25:

"And he brought us out from thence to bring us in and give us the land which he promised to our fathers. The Lord commanded us to keep all these statutes, and to fear the Lord our God, that it may go well with us all our days, and that he may preserve our lives, as it is this day. And we shall have righteousness, if we observe to do all these commandments before the Lord our God, as he hath commanded us.

God had brought them out of the land of Egypt. His purpose was to bring them to the promised land, which was a place of blessing. And so it is in the case of our salvation. God has saved us from death, sin and judgment. He has brought us into the body of Christ, which is the church, into the place of blessing, into communion with Himself, and finally He will take us to heaven, where our salvation will then be complete. Let us remember that St. Paul said in Romans 4:25: *He was delivered for our transgressions, and was raised again for our justification. He has declared us righteous.* He is our righteousness, so that we may stand before God complete. As happened to the ancient people in the Old Testament, those of us who are believers in Jesus Christ, He has delivered us from a place of bondage to a place of blessing. And that experience can be shared by you, dear listener. Every human being, is tremendously far from God, in a state of slavery because of the sin of his human nature, and with an attitude of natural rebellion that leads to ultimate perdition. But God is accessible and has already provided salvation, liberation, through Jesus Christ, the one who paid our debt with God. He himself is the way to God, and the arms that were opened when he was crucified, are now open in an attitude of invitation, for all who believe in Jesus Christ as their Savior.

Deuteronomy 7:1-8:9

I n our study of the book of Deuteronomy, we come to chapter 7. But before entering into the study of this chapter, let us add something. We said at the end of our previous episode, that God has saved us from death, sin and judgment. He brought us into the body of Christ, which is the church, into the place of blessing, into communion with Himself, and finally He will lead us to heaven to culminate His work of salvation.

The Lord Jesus was delivered up for our trespasses and raised for our justification, as the apostle Paul told us in his letter to the Romans 4:25. *He was raised for our justification, that we might be complete before Him.* Today, then, and in the first place, every Christian can say the following: He has saved me. We already have eternal life. We already stand before God because of the righteousness and merits of our Savior. The apostle John in his first letter, 5:11 and 12, said: "And this is the record, that God hath given unto us eternal life; and this life is in his Son. He that hath the Son hath life; he that hath not the Son of God hath not life."

The second thing the Christian can say today is: I am being saved. God is at work in my life; guiding it and conforming it more and more to the image of His Son. The apostle Paul says in his letter to the Philippians 2:12,13: *"Work out your salvation with fear and trembling, for it is God who works in you both to will and to do of His good pleasure."* He is working out the results of salvation in our lives.

Thirdly, the Christian can say: It will save me. No one should be discouraged by looking at himself or others, by reflecting on his own or others' lack of spiritual evolution. For God has not yet finished

56

His work in believers. The apostle John told us in his first letter 3:2: *"Beloved, now are we the sons of God, and it doth not yet appear what we shall be: but we know that, when he shall appear, we shall be like him; for we shall see him as he is."* How true that is, dear hearer! God has not finished His work in any of us. And when He appears in all His glory, we shall be like Him. And we turn now to,

Deuteronomy 7

We find here the instructions for the conquest of the earth. First, let us consider,

Israel's separation from other nations

Let us read the first two verses of this chapter 7 of Deuteronomy:

"When the Lord, your God, has brought you into the land which you are about to enter to take it, and has driven out from before you many nations: the Hittite, the Girgashite, the Amorite, the Canaanite, the Perizzite, the Hivite, and the Jebusite, seven nations greater and mightier than you, and the Lord, your God, has delivered them to you and you have defeated them, you shall utterly destroy them. Thou shalt make no covenant with them, neither shalt thou have mercy on them."

Now, this is very severe language. Recall that God had said, "Thou shalt not kill". In that commandment the verb ratsach referred to personal grudge; personal hatred that leads to murder. Here it is a different word, which is charam and means to dedicate or consecrate (to God or to destruction). Here he commanded them directly to destroy those who lived on the earth.

Let us continue reading verses 3 and 4

"Thou shalt not intermarry with them, thou shalt not give thy daughter to their son, nor take their daughter for thy son. For he will put away your son from me, who would serve other gods. Then the anger of the Lord will be kindled against you, and he will destroy you very quickly."

We have here the reason for God's commandment. These people were being consumed by venereal diseases. If the Israelites had intermarried with them, they would have destroyed the race. Moses did not understand much about pathogenic microbes; but God knows a great deal about them. These people were continually contaminating and infecting themselves, due to a way of life devoid of the most elementary moral principles and respect for basic human rights. And therefore, God expelled them from the earth. Not only that, but these people were idolatrous and would have led Israel into idolatry. Therefore, God told them that they must completely destroy their altars and their images. All this destructive influence was to be totally removed. No one knows human nature better than the Creator. His work of salvation began already in the Old Testament and He knew well who could participate in His purpose to restore the human race to its proper dignity and quality of life, and who would persist in its self-destruction.

God pronounced a solemn warning. If they intermarried with them and if they returned to worship other gods, God would drive them out of the land as well. And yet God made it clear to Israel that He was the God of love. He gave them these commandments because He loved them. Let us continue reading verses 6 through 8 of this 7th chapter of Deuteronomy:

"For you are a holy people to the Lord your God; the Lord your God has chosen you to be a special people to him, above all the peoples that are on the earth. Not because you were the most numerous of all peoples did the Lord love you and choose you, for you were the least of all peoples, but because the Lord loved you and was willing to keep the oath which he swore to your fathers; therefore the Lord brought you out with a mighty hand, and redeemed you out of bondage from the hand of Pharaoh king of Egypt."

You will recall that God told them in the book of Exodus that He had heard the cry of their pain. That groaning found an answer in God's heart because He loved them and, for that reason, He freed them from slavery. And He continued to repeat to them to obey His commandments. For what should be man's response to God's love? Obedience. Let us read verses 9 to 11:

"Know therefore that the Lord, your God, is God, a faithful God, who keeps covenant and mercy to those who love him and keep his commandments, even to a thousand generations, but who gives his due, in his own person, to him who hates him, destroying him; to him who hates him, he does not delay to repay him in his own person. Keep therefore the commandments, statutes, and judgments, which I command you this day to do."

God would bless any people who responded to God with an attitude of obedience. Let us continue reading verses 12 and 13:

"Because thou hast heard these decrees, and hast kept them, and done them, the Lord thy God will keep with thee the covenant and the mercy which he sware unto thy fathers. He will love you, bless you and multiply you, bless the fruit of your womb and the fruit of your ground, your grain, your new wine, your oil, the increase of your herds and the flocks of your flocks, in the land which he swore to your fathers to give you."

How wonderful it would have been if Israel had believed God. He told them all these things to encourage them. He promised them victory. Let us turn now to verses 17 and 18:

"If you say in your heart, 'These nations are far more numerous than I, how can I exterminate them,' do not be afraid of them. Remember well what the Lord your God did to Pharaoh and to all Egypt."

God's faithfulness in the past was to serve as an encouragement to them for the future. Is it not precisely the same with us, dear listener? Let us turn now to verses 21 and 22 of this chapter 7 of Deuteronomy:

"Do not faint before them, for the Lord your God is in the midst of you, O great and awesome God. The Lord, your God, will drive out these nations from before you little by little; you will not be able to wipe them out at once, lest the wild beasts of the field multiply against you."

Here we see God's wisdom: He was thinking of their safety, knowing that if that population were suddenly destroyed, wild animals would occupy the land. Let us now read verse 23:

"But the Lord, your God, will deliver them up before you, and will cause them great destruction until they are destroyed."

All these nations were to be driven from the earth, and utterly destroyed because of their practices, which led to their own extermination. Now, we cannot say that God had not been patient with them. Even in Genesis 15:16, God had told Abraham that his descendants would not return to the land until the fourth generation. "For the wickedness of the Amorites shall not yet have reached its height." God gave these nations 430 years to see if they would turn from their sins to God. How much longer should God have prolonged His mercy and patience? God gave them a time of mercy that lasted about 430 years. But, then the cup of wickedness was filled, and God's judgment descended upon them. Therefore, it is better not to have false compassion for those nations. Rather, let us learn from these events. God is a God of mercy and love, both in the Old Testament and in the New Testament.

And so we conclude our study of Deuteronomy chapter 7.

Deuteronomy 8:1-9

———

Theme: God's past dealings with human beings provide security for the future.

In this discourse of repetition of the law, one would think that the great emphasis would be on law and obedience, but we are seeing that the emphasis was on love and obedience.

You will recall that in chapter 7, we learned that the Lord did not love the Israelites because they were many. In reality they were few. Israel had never been a large nation, numerically speaking, so what would be the response to that kind of love? The response had to be obedience! God would bless anyone who responded to His love. And that response to His love had to be obedience.

We now come to the section dealing with religious and national regulations. This section includes this chapter 8 until chapter 21. Let us read then, the first verse of this chapter 8 of Deuteronomy, which begins the paragraph entitled,

The memory of the past was to stimulate obedience

"You shall observe to do every commandment which I command you this day, that you may live, and multiply, and go in to possess the land which the Lord promised with an oath to your fathers."

Here was the new generation, on the eastern side of the Jordan River. They were ready to cross over to the other side and enter the land with much trepidation and hope. As Moses was preparing them to enter the land, he encouraged them to obey God. Let us continue with verse 2:

> *"Thou shalt remember all the way by which the Lord thy God hath brought thee these forty years in the wilderness, to afflict thee, to try thee, to know what was in thine heart, whether thou wouldest keep his commandments or no."*

God wanted them to remember the past. They were to see that in the past, God had dealt with them, testing and preparing them....

And God wants us to remember our past as well. Paul expressed it for the believer, in his letter to the Philippians 1:6, as follows: "...being confident of this, that he which hath begun a good work in you will perform it until the day of Jesus Christ." We must remember that God has guided us and blessed us. Is this not true of you, dear listener? Can you not say that God has guided you to this very hour? If He has done so in the past, He will continue to do so in the future. These memories are for our encouragement; to give us assurance for the future.

Now, why did God test the Israelites in the wilderness? It was to humble them and to demonstrate what was truly in their hearts. That explains why God tests you and me. Sometimes it's like he puts us in the oven and makes it really hot. What for? You say. Well, to test us and to humble us. Remember that the Christian is not exempt from pride or from developing excessive self-confidence. We can easily observe the boastfulness and pride with which man walks the earth today. Therefore, God must take His people and cause them to pass through trials in order to humble them.

Did you know that the tests really prove the quality of the metal? Tests will reveal whether a person is truly a child of God or not. That is why it is often difficult to know if a believer is genuine or not. A person who has been tested is someone who can be trusted. Let's continue reading verse 3 of this chapter 8 of Deuteronomy:

"He afflicted you, and made you hungry, and fed you with manna, food that neither you nor your fathers had known, to make you know that man shall not live by bread alone, but by everything that proceeds out of the mouth of the Lord shall man live."

Our Lord quoted this verse when He was tempted in the wilderness. We find this in Matthew 4:4 and also in Luke 4:4. If the Lord Jesus had not quoted this verse, it is likely that we would have overlooked the great spiritual lesson here.

God has been kind to us. He has blessed us with material things, in many ways. The important lesson is that God gives us those things, so that we see that there is a spiritual wealth, and that wealth is the Word of God. The Word of God is what today constitutes the true wealth for the child of God. Let's continue with verse 4:

"The dress you wore never grew old, nor has your foot swollen in these forty years."

Then he says: "Not even your foot has swollen in these forty years". A doctor who was also a missionary, once explained that in a country in the East where he lived; the people had a fixed diet, without variations. They did not receive all the vitamins they needed, and therefore show symptoms of a disease called beriberi, caused by a lack of vitamin B1 in the diet, and one of the symptoms of which is swelling of the feet. Now, the Israelites did receive all the vitamins and food that the body needed. What did the Israelites eat for forty years? Well, they ate the manna. God gave them the manna to eat, which was a wonderful, miraculous food. It provided all the food they needed for the proper nutrition and health of their bodies.

Spiritual manna is a description of the Word of God. It is a wonderful food that will supply all your needs. Here in the episode The Fountain of Life, we admire how the letters received prove this reality. We received many, many letters and among them we can find the letter of that listener who told us that he was going through a great affliction, and that one day we talked about a certain chapter that brought comfort to his heart. Another told us that he was far from God, in sin, and that he had become a cold and indifferent person. But a particular passage from God's Word enabled him to restore his relationship with God. Another wrote to tell us that he heard the episode and that God saved him by receiving the Lord Jesus Christ as his personal Savior. the Bible will meet your individual needs, whatever they may be.

Now, God promised temporal blessings to the nation of Israel if they would serve Him. Let us read verses 5 through 9 of this chapter 8 of Deuteronomy:

"Know in your heart that as a man chastises his son, so the Lord your God chastises you. Thou shalt therefore keep the commandments of the Lord thy God, walking in his ways and fearing him. For the Lord thy God bringeth thee into the good land, a land of brooks and waters and fountains and springs, springing up in valleys and mountains; a land of wheat and barley, of vines and fig trees and pomegranates; a land of olive trees and oil and honey; a land wherein thou shalt eat bread without scarcity, and wherein thou shalt lack nothing; a land whose stones are of iron, and out of whose mountains thou shalt bring forth copper."

God does not give this promise to Christians today. And we would like you to note this well. There is an unbalanced notion that if you are faithful, God will prosper you with temporal goods. that is not true. God promised to prosper Israel in the land. But, He did not promise to prosper the Christian with the material goods of this world.

A few moments ago we compared the manna that God provided to those people in the desert with the Word of God. We would like to conclude by affirming that the Bible, the Word of God, presents us with Jesus Christ, the Word of God incarnate, who lived among us, left us His teachings, died on a cross for us and rose again. We have said today that the response to love should be obedience. The response that He asks of you today is that you believe in the Lord Jesus Christ, in order to be saved. And Jesus Himself, from the pages of the Holy Scriptures, reminds us of His invitation, recorded in John 6:35, when He said; I am the bread of life. He who comes to me shall never hunger, and he who believes in me shall never thirst.

Deuteronomy 8:10-9:18

———

Referring to verses 5 through 9 of this chapter, in our previous episode we said that God did not give this promise of material prosperity to Christians. There is a misconception that if you are faithful, God will prosper you with temporal goods. God promised to prosper Israel in the land. But, He did not promise to prosper the Christian with the material goods of this world. The promise to the Christian is: "Blessed be the God and Father of our Lord Jesus Christ, who has blessed us with every spiritual blessing in the heavenly places in Christ" (Ephesians 1:3). He has promised us spiritual blessings. There is no verse that promises temporal blessings to the child of God today.

Let us also add that God does not promise temporal blessings, but He does add them. And furthermore, we should be thankful that He supplies our needs, for He knows our real needs, beyond what we think we need. And we also want to say that some of God's choicest children have been blessed with spiritual blessings, but not with material prosperity. We believe that such persons seem to be the happiest, and seem to do more for the work of God than any others. They have been a blessing to the cause of Christ in the world.

We want to point out that one of the major distinctions between the nation of Israel in the Old Testament and the Church in the New Testament is that God promised temporal blessings to Israel, and promises us every spiritual blessing. Keeping this distinction in mind will avoid a great deal of grief among God's people. It will cause very many of God's children to rejoice and not fall into despondency or depression.

Let us begin, then, our reading today, in Deuteronomy chapter 8, verses 10 and 11:

"There you shall eat and be satisfied, and bless the Lord, your God, for the good land he has given you. Take heed that you do not forget the Lord, your God, to keep the commandments, decrees, and statutes which I command you this day."

Here we see that he continued to express his warnings to Israel, in light of the coming times of prosperity. Let us read verses 14 to 16:

"Let not your heart be proud and forget the Lord, your God, who brought you out of the land of Egypt, out of the house of bondage; who made you walk through a great and dreadful wilderness, full of poisonous serpents and scorpions; who in a land of thirst and without water brought you water out of the rock of flint; who sustained you with manna in the wilderness, food which your fathers had not known, afflicting you and testing you, that in the end he might do you good."

In John 14:2, 3, the Lord said: "I go to prepare a place for you. And if I go and prepare a place for you, I will come again, and receive you unto myself; that where I am, there ye may be also". This is the hope of the child of God today. Christ will come to take us out of this world. Israel's hope was in this world. That is the difference. If you try to mix up these promises, it could cause confusion. If one lets the Bible state its claims, both in similarities and differences, we will see that God has been very specific in pronouncing His promises. Let us continue reading verses 17 and 18 of this chapter 8 of Deuteronomy:

"and say in your heart, 'My power and the might of my hand have brought me this wealth;' but remember the Lord your God, for it is he who gives you the power to acquire wealth, to confirm the covenant which he swore to your fathers, as he does today."

When the nation of Israel was in the promised land and the Lord prospered them, then we would know that they were obeying God. When they did not prosper in that land, it would be an indication that they were not obeying God. And as we observe these people today, their spiritual condition is evident to us. Let us continue reading verses 19 and 20:

"But if you forget the Lord your God, and go after other gods, and serve them, and bow down to them, I testify against you this day, that you shall surely perish. Like the nations which the Lord will destroy before you, so shall you perish, because you have not obeyed the voice of the Lord your God."

This was God's warning to the Israelites. He promised to bless them if they obeyed him. If they were not obedient, he would treat them as he treated those nations that were in that land before them. The truth is that God treated the Israelites even worse than He treated the other nations that lived in that land. Do you know why? Because the people of Israel had been given a greater revelation. And that knowledge created a responsibility before God. And so we come to,

Deuteronomy 9:1-18

———

Theme: God knew Israel - Their past had not been good.

God was examining the past of the nation of Israel. God knew these people and knew that their past was not good. God had not saved the people of Israel because they were good. He did not call them because they were a remarkable nation. They were not.

God has not saved us because we are outstanding, superior, or good. The only kind of human beings God saves are the bad ones.

God saves us, because we are evil. Because he knows our lost condition. Let us now read verses 1 and 2 of this chapter 9 of Deuteronomy:

> *"Hear, O Israel: thou art this day going over Jordan, to go in to dispossess nations more numerous and mightier than thou, cities great and walled up to heaven, a people great and high, the children of the Anakims, of whom thou hast knowledge, and of whom thou hast heard say, Who shall stand before the children of Anak?"*

God gave a report concerning the land, which was worse than the report the spies had given on their return from the land. God knew the land and knew who was in it. However, God had commanded them to go in. But, they had refused to enter because they did not believe God. God knew that those who resided there were giants. He knew all the difficulties and had promised to enter the land with them.

It was Martin Luther who said: "One with God, constitutes a majority". if you are with God, you are with the majority. Actually, Christians belong to the minority group here in this world. But, there is something the world does not know. By being with God, we are in the majority. Let us not forget this. Let us now read verse 3 of Deuteronomy 9:

"Understand, therefore, this day, that it is the Lord, your God, who passes before you like a consuming fire, who will destroy and humble them in your presence. Thou shalt cast them out and destroy them at once, as the Lord hath said unto thee."

God assumed the responsibility of expelling them from the earth. God is the owner of the earth. He is the Creator. He has the right to do this. God is the Sovereign Creator; we are the creatures. Verse 4 says:

"When the Lord, your God, has cast them out from before you, do not say in your heart, 'Because of my righteousness the Lord has brought me to possess this land,' for because of the wickedness of these nations the Lord casts them out from before you.'"

God said that he was driving the other nations out of the land, because those nations were wicked. And not because the nation he was bringing into the land was a righteous nation. And God clarified this very well. Let's read verse 5 of this Deuteronomy chapter 9:

"Not for your righteousness nor for the uprightness of your heart do you go in to possess their land, but for the wickedness of these nations the Lord, your God, drives them out from before you, and to confirm the word which the Lord swore to your fathers Abraham, Isaac, and Jacob."

Here it was clear that God did not deliver Israel because they were a charming people. He knew from the beginning that they were a stubborn and obstinate people. But He had heard their cry from Egypt. if you recognize that you are a sinner and need a Savior, then you will have to cry out to Him for salvation, and He will hear you. And He will hear you, and do you know why? not because of who you are or His goodness, but because of Christ. If you turn to Him by faith, He will save you. Verse 6 adds:

"Therefore know that the Lord your God does not give you this good land for your righteousness, for you are a stubborn people."

In other words, transferring this principle to our present situation, God does not save you because you are good. We are all sinners. And He saves us by the merits of Christ, not by our own merits. If you believe that God will find in you something worthy of salvation, you will be disappointed. God knows you perfectly well and says that He will in no way find righteousness in you. It is for Christ's sake that God saves us, and God finds everything we need in Him. In this passage from the book of Deuteronomy is found the seed of the Gospel of God's grace.

Let us read verse 7 of Deuteronomy 9, which begins the paragraph entitled,

Israel's past failure

"Remember, do not forget that you provoked the Lord, your God, to anger in the wilderness; from the day you came out of the land of Egypt, until you entered this place, you have been rebellious to the Lord."

Moses reminded them of their past history, and referred specifically to the time when they made the golden calf. In Exodus 32:4 we read the following words: "and he (Aaron) received them from their hands," referring to the golden earrings. The women and men also took off their gold earrings and gave them to Aaron. These gold earrings were a sign of idolatry. They usually wore them in one ear only. These people had fallen very quickly into idolatry. Aaron took the gold earrings, melted the gold and chiseled it into the shape of a calf. Then they all said, "Israel, this is your God who brought you out of Egypt!" God made them remember this. God made them remember this grave fact again in Psalm 106:19 "They made a calf in Horeb, they bowed down to a molten image." God required them to remember, but they forgot. Accordingly, verse 8 says:

"In Horeb you provoked the Lord to anger, and the Lord was angry with you to destroy you."

And Moses continued with his narration of that episode. Let us read verse 12.

"And he said unto me, Arise, come down quickly from hence; for the people whom thou broughtest out of Egypt have corrupted themselves. They have quickly turned aside from the way which I commanded them, and have made themselves a molten image."

At the same time that they were making the golden calf, Moses was on the mountain receiving the commandments, and two of these commandments prohibited precisely the idolatry that the people were practicing: "You shall have no other gods before me. You shall not make for yourself a graven image or any other image". Notice that God said to Moses: *"They are your people. You brought them out of Egypt.* And Moses would answer him later. Let us now read verse 13:

"The Lord also said to me, 'I have watched this people and have seen that they are a stubborn people."

The Lord repeated these words again. He knew all along that Israel was a stubborn people. He knows you and me too, and He could probably say the same about us. And the Lord went on to say in verse 14:

"Let me destroy them and blot out their name from under heaven, and I will set you over a nation strong and far more numerous than they."

This must have been a temptation for Moses, but he resisted it. His plea on behalf of Israel was recounted in Exodus 33:12-17. Moses would not go up to the Promised Land without the presence of the Lord. He said, "If your presence is not to accompany us, do not bring us up from here." Moses identified himself with the people. And when he came down from the mountain, he saw what the people had done. Let us read verse 16:

> *"I looked and saw that you had sinned against the Lord, your God:*
> *you had made yourselves a molten calf, turning aside quickly from*
> *the way which the Lord had appointed for you."*

At that very moment when God was giving them the commandments, they were turning away from Him. And yet they said they were going to obey Him. We suppose that people can be more false in the area of religion than in any other aspect. This attitude is characteristic of human nature. Even sometimes people who appear to be sincere can adopt attitudes of pretense. We all need to pray the following prayer of the psalmist in Psalm 139:23, 24: "Search me, O God, and know my heart; test me and know my thoughts; see if there is any wicked way in me, and lead me in the way everlasting.

St. Paul had these words of admonition for believers, in 2 Corinthians 13:5: "Examine yourselves, to see whether ye be in the faith; prove your own selves: or know ye not your own selves? know ye not that Jesus Christ is in you? unless ye have failed the test!" Examine yourselves to see whether you are in the faith, or not. We believe, and preach the security of the believer, friend who hears us. We believe that the believer is secure, but we also believe and preach the insecurity of the one who pretends, or who is a hypocrite. Each of us needs to examine his heart. Let's go back to our Deuteronomy chapter 9 and read verses 17 and 18:

"Then I took the two tablets, threw them out of my two hands, and broke them before your eyes. Then I fell down before the Lord, and as I did before, for forty days and forty nights I ate no bread and drank no water, because of all the sin that you had committed by doing evil in the sight of the Lord to provoke him to anger."

Now, notice that Moses knew God. The psalmist said in Psalm 103:7: *"He made known His ways unto Moses, and His works unto the children of Israel.* The Israelites saw the smoking mountain, they saw God's judgment, they saw His glory, but they did not know Him. Moses did know Him! Moses knew His plans, His purposes.

Moses understood two things about God, which are revealed here. They are paradoxical, but not contradictory.

Moses knew that God hates sin. Let us tell you that today, we have not the remotest conception of how God hates sin, nor how He intends to punish it. Moses knelt before God and fasted and cried out to God for 40 days and 40 nights. Moses knew God's ways. He knew how God abhors sin.

It seems that today the average Christian does not seem to realize how God is bothered by sin in his life. God will never overlook sin; he will deal with that sin in his life and in the life of each of us. Sometimes the judgment is very severe. God abhors sin and punishes it.

Moses also knew God's mercy. Moses turned to God because he trusted in His mercy. God punishes sin, but we do not understand how wonderful He is. He is so gracious. He extends mercy to the sinner. He has extended His mercy to you, of that we are sure. We know that He has extended His mercy to each one of us. And the Lord extended His mercy to Moses and to Israel.

Some people have become very distant from God and His demands for the life and dignity of human beings. One of the consequences they experience is low self-esteem. And they avoid facing this situation for various reasons such as, for example, considering that God would not receive them or, simply, that He could not raise them to the full human dignity they would like to achieve. if this is your case, if in any way what we have said is close to your personal situation, as we say goodbye until our next meeting, we would like to remind you of the words of a psalm, and we hope that these ancient words will not seem remote, distant to you. Although they were addressed to many, many people down through the centuries, they were also spoken personally to you and so we wish you to receive them. Psalm 34:18 says, The Lord is near to save those whose hearts are broken and who have lost hope.

Surely you want to rebuild your life; to rebuild what was broken and recover what was lost because of sin and human wickedness. Does this seem impossible to you? No, it does not. It is not. God has already done everything necessary to save you through Jesus Christ and His death on the cross. We invite you to accept this reality by faith. We invite you to prove that He delivers, that He transforms, that He provides life in abundance, quality life here on earth, and eternal life beyond death.

Deuteronomy 9:19-11:32

———

We ended our previous episode by stating that Moses had turned to God because he trusted in His mercy. Although God punishes sin, we fail to understand how wonderful He is. For God extends His mercy to you and me, just as He offered His mercy to Israel. So let us begin our reading today in Deuteronomy 9:19:

"For I feared because of the fury and wrath with which the Lord was angry with you, even to the point of wanting to destroy you. But the Lord heard me once more."

God did not extend His mercy to Moses because of who he was. God did not hear Moses' plea because he was the deliverer, the leader of the Israelites. Paul clarified this in Romans 9:15, which says, *"For unto Moses he saith, I will have mercy upon whom I will have mercy, and I will have compassion on whom I will have compassion."* God is sovereign and He sovereignly extends His mercy, how wonderful He is! You and I cannot fully understand these two characteristics of God: His hatred of sin and His mercy. Let us continue reading verses 20 and 21:

"The Lord was also very angry with Aaron, even to the point of wanting to destroy him. I also prayed for Aaron at that time. Then I took the object of your sin, the calf which you had made, and I burned it in the fire and broke it in pieces, grinding it very fine, until it was ground to powder, and I threw the powder into the brook that ran down from the mountain."

If this incident were not so tragic, it would be funny. Moses made the Israelites drink their idol. Let us now read verse 24:

"Ye have been rebels unto the Lord from the day that I knew you."

This was the summary. There was never even a day in which these Israelites were really faithful to God. What a picture! We are prone to criticize them, aren't we? But what shall we say of many Christians today, who boast of the truthfulness and legitimacy of their faith and beliefs, and seem to be spiritually asleep? Verse 25 of Deuteronomy chapter 9 says:

> *"So I fell down before the Lord; forty days and forty nights I was prostrate, because the Lord said that he would destroy you."*

This occurred after they refused to enter the land of Kadesh-barnea. Moses knew God. Moses knew that God judges sin. Let us read verses 26 to 29:

> *"And I prayed unto the Lord, saying, O Lord, destroy not thy people, the inheritance which thou hast redeemed by thy greatness, which thou hast brought forth out of Egypt with a mighty hand. Remember your servants Abraham, Isaac and Jacob; do not look upon the hardness of this people, their wickedness or their sin, lest those in the land from which you brought us out say, 'Because the Lord could not bring them into the land which he promised them, or because he hated them, he brought them out to kill them in the wilderness. They are thy people, the inheritance which thou hast brought forth by thy great power and by thy stretched out arm."*

Moses knew how to pray, if only we knew how to pray as he prayed! Remember that in verse 12 God said: "because your people whom you brought out of Egypt have corrupted themselves". Now, imagine Moses telling God that he had made a mistake. Moses said, "They are not my people but Yours. I did not bring them out of Egypt but You did. They are Yours." Moses reminded God that the inhabitants of the Promised Land would believe that God had been able to bring them out of Egypt but had not been able to bring Israel into the land. That kind of prayer did move God's hand. And here, at last, were the people of Israel, ready to enter the land, which reveals to us that Moses knew how to pray. And so we come to,

Deuteronomy 10

———

Theme: God had sent Israel to Egypt; And God brought them out of Egypt.

Moses in his supplication reminded God that the children of Israel belonged to Him, that they were God's inheritance. They were God's inheritance. He would not destroy them because of their sin but rather, in His goodness, He gave them again the Ten Commandments written by Himself. Let us read the first two verses of this chapter 10:

> *At that time the Lord said to me, "Make for yourself two tables of stone like the first ones, and come up to me on the mountain. Make you also an ark of wood. I will write on those tablets the words that were on the first tablets which you broke, and you shall put them in the ark."*

Moses came down from the mountain with the tablets and put them in the ark. Then the children of Israel continued their journey. Let us read verses 8 and 9:

> *"At that time the LORD set apart the tribe of Levi to bear the ark of the covenant of the LORD, to stand before the LORD, and to minister unto him, and to bless in his name, even unto this day. Therefore Levi had no part nor inheritance among his brethren: the Lord is his inheritance, as the Lord thy God said unto him."*

There are great spiritual lessons here for us. Just as Levi was the priestly tribe, today, the Church is, spiritually speaking, a kingdom of priests. That is, every believer in Jesus Christ is a priest. (I am not a Roman Catholic priest, but I am still a "Catholic" priest, as is every believer in Christ, in the sense that "Catholic" means "universal"). The New

Testament priest had to offer himself to God for worship, intercession and service (Romans 12:1, 2), AND as a priest, he had to exercise a gift, according to 1 Corinthians 12. And every believer, as a priest, has a gift to exercise in the church.

The ancient tribe of Levi was not to have any material inheritance. God Himself was their inheritance. God had promised to give the land, a certain tract of land, to the other tribes. And when he blessed them, it was a temporary blessing. But he did not promise that to Levi. This is also the position of the believer today. For us today, as in the case of Levi, our inheritance is in God. We have been blessed with every spiritual blessing in the heavenly places in Christ. Let us read verses 12 and 13 of this 10th chapter of Deuteronomy.

"Now therefore, Israel, what does the Lord, your God, require of you but to fear the Lord, your God, to walk in all His ways, to love and serve the Lord, your God, with all your heart and with all your soul, to keep the commandments of the Lord and His statutes, which I command you this day, that you may prosper?"

If the Israelites had kept the law, they would have been blessed. When they violated the law, judgment came upon them. For 1500 years, God demonstrated through Israel to the world, to you and to me, that He cannot save people through the law. The Israelites, under the most favorable circumstances, in a land and social system regulated by law, were unable to obey that law. If it was not possible for them to fulfill it, we have to admit that we are not able to fulfill it either. We should be thankful that God saves people today by His grace. In fact, grace has always been His method. In the Old Testament He never saved anyone by means of the Law. People were saved by grace, by His mercy, which He applied to them, anxiously awaiting the coming of Christ to die on a cross for the forgiveness of their sins. (They had to demonstrate their faith and manifest their love for God by their obedience to the Law). Let us now turn to verses 18 and 19:

"Who doeth justice to the fatherless and widow, who loveth the sojourner also, and giveth him bread and raiment. Ye shall therefore love the stranger, because ye were strangers in the land of Egypt."

God demonstrated His love for the orphan and the stranger, and so should the Israelites. They had to remember that they had been strangers in the land of Egypt. And verse 20 adds:

"The Lord thy God shalt thou fear, him only shalt thou serve, him shalt thou follow, and in his name shalt thou swear."

This is the same statement we find in Deuteronomy chapter 6, verse 13. Our Lord quoted these words when answering Satan in the temptation episode. The Lord Jesus knew the book of Deuteronomy well, as probably did all the Israelites of that time. Let us now read verse 22 of this 10th chapter of Deuteronomy.

"With seventy persons your fathers went down to Egypt, but now the Lord has caused you to multiply as the stars of heaven."

God's evident blessing remained upon them. He had sent them to Egypt. He had brought them out of Egypt. God was responsible and He did not mind taking that responsibility.

Deuteronomy 11:1-32

———

Theme: the promised land was not like Egypt; the principle for the occupation of the land.

God spoke to them in this passage about the land they were about to enter. The promised land was in no way like Egypt. And God would communicate to them the principles required to occupy the land. Let us first consider a paragraph entitled:

A call for commitment

Let us begin our consideration of this 11th chapter of Deuteronomy by reading the first verse:

"Thou shalt therefore love the Lord thy God, and keep his statutes, and his judgments, and his judgments, and his commandments, and his commandments, all the days."

Here we emphasize that the response to God's love was obedience. Let us turn to verses 8 and 9:

"Keep therefore all the commandments which I command you this day, that ye may be strengthened, and go in to possess the land whither ye go over to take it, and that your days may be prolonged upon the land, of which the Lord sware unto your fathers to give it unto them and to their seed, a land flowing with milk and honey."

They were used to irrigating the land back in Egypt. But this new land was rich in agriculture and livestock. Verse 10 says:

"The land into which you are going to enter to take it is not like the land of Egypt, from whence you came out, where you sowed your seed and watered with your foot, like a vegetable garden."

When we visited Egypt, we were told that the amount of rain that falls during the year is equivalent to just over 25 cm. Now, that is a very low amount of rain. However, there is a place in the Hawaiian Islands where the amount of rain that falls during the year is equivalent to more than 2.5 m. What a difference! And a half. What a difference! Let's read verses 11 through 15, which begin a paragraph entitled,

The principle for the occupation and possession of the Promised Land

"The land that you are about to enter to take it is a land of mountains and meadows, a land that drinks the waters of the rain of heaven, a land that the Lord your God cares for. The eyes of the Lord your God are always upon it from the beginning of the year to the end. If you will carefully obey the commandments which I command you this day, loving the Lord, your God, and serving him with all your heart and with all your soul, I will give the rain to your land in its season, the early rain and the latter rain, and you shall gather in your grain, your wine and your oil. I will also give grass in your field for your cattle, and you shall eat your fill."

The land into which the Israelites were to enter would be somewhat difficult to irrigate because it was mountainous. They did not have adequate means to irrigate at that time, and the land would depend on rain. God did this for a purpose. He put them in a land that had to depend on Him for rain. This circumstance would bring the people closer to God.

The reason why the land is desolate today is because God's judgment is upon it, as we will see in this book of Deuteronomy. The moment it is watered, the desert blooms like a rose, because what it needs is water and even today, they have difficulties there with the lack of water. God told them that they would depend on the rain. If they obeyed him, he would bless them with rain from heaven, with the autumn and spring rains. Looking at that land today, you can see the spiritual condition of the people.

In a society as affluent as the one we have today, where things are obtained very easily, we fear that people assume that God has absolutely nothing to do with it. We don't understand why people believe that if things are easily obtained, they are the ones who have achieved it, and that if things are obtained with difficulty, then it is God who has to do with that situation. God is the one who provides for all physical needs, whether things come easily or with difficulty. He is still the one who provides. Verse 22 says:

"For if you carefully keep all these commandments which I command you to do, and if you love the Lord your God, walking in all his ways and following him."

Here we have precisely the beginning of the occupation and possession of the land. Let us also read verses 24 and 25:

"Every place that the sole of your foot shall tread upon shall be yours: from the wilderness to Lebanon, from the river Euphrates to the western sea shall be your territory. No one shall stand before you; fear and dread of you shall the Lord your God put upon all the land that you shall tread upon, as he has said to you."

We will see this principle of occupation again in the book of Joshua, where it will have special emphasis. You will observe that the land was a gift from God. He had given them a land that was more extensive than any other they had occupied. It stretched from the Euphrates River to the Mediterranean Sea, and from Lebanon all the way south to the wilderness they had crossed. It was approximately 777,000 square kilometers. They had never lived on more than 77,000 square kilometers of such land; not even at the time when the kingdom reached its apogee under the reigns of David and Solomon.

Let us take note of the phrase: Every place whereon the sole of your foot shall tread shall be yours. The land had been given to them by God and was theirs, but they failed to tread it, claim it and enjoy it. Later, God would tell Joshua the same thing. He told him that the land was right there before them, and that it belonged to Israel. But He told him that they had to go in and go through it. They had to take possession of it.

Why is there such a difference among believers today? Some Christians simply sit on the sidelines or watch from the sidelines, uncommitted and very poor spiritually speaking. Others are fabulously rich, also spiritually speaking. God clearly stated that He has blessed all believers with all kinds of spiritual blessings through Christ. Some believers have claimed those blessings and others have not. Some believers enjoy those blessings and some do not. It is a matter of appropriating what we already possess. Let us read verse 26:

> *"Behold, I set before you this day the blessing and the curse."*

That is, the Israelites were commanded to obey. Obedience was the crucial, the most important part of this matter. Let us continue reading verse 27:

> *"the blessing, if you obey the commandments of the Lord your God, which I command you this day."*

Obedience has today taken a back seat. Now, we do believe in God's grace and preach it. We are saved by grace, we are kept by grace, and we grow spiritually in maturity by God's grace. We will get to heaven by God's grace. When we have been there a few thousand years, it will still be a result of God's grace. But, there are great spiritual blessings today, which you will lose if you are not obedient to Him. Jesus told us that if we love Him, obey His commandments. Obedience offers a personal, wonderful and glorious relationship with God. God will bless obedience.

The opposite is also true. Disobedience brings the curse.

Let us read verse 28:

> *"and the curse, if you do not obey the commandments of the Lord your God, and turn aside from the way which I command you this day, to go after other gods which you have not known."*

You will observe that the great issue over which God implored Israel was idolatry. There was always the danger that they would turn away from the Lord their God and fall back under the control of idolatry.

Let us remember, in conclusion, that everything that interferes or comes between man and God, everything that draws our attention away from the need to maintain a priority relationship with God, the Creator and the Lord Jesus Christ, the Savior, leads to a contemporary form of idolatry, which continues to be a form of sin against God, and which, by turning away from Him, separates man from the principles of life, from his own salvation, from human dignity and respect for his fellow man. But the opposite attitude is like finding "The Source of Life". It is to reach God through the Lord Jesus Christ. It is to discover another way of living this existence in the world, and it is to receive eternal life. It is to turn over a new leaf and begin a totally different life. As St. Paul said in 2 Corinthians 5:17, *"He who is united to Christ is a new person. The old things have passed away; they have become new".*

Deuteronomy 12:1-13:16

Continuing our study in the book of Deuteronomy, we come to chapter 12. In this chapter we will see that Israel would have only one place to worship in the promised land. Later in Israel's history, God would choose Jerusalem for the place where the temple would be built. The Israelites were to go there to worship God. Now, why didn't God allow worship in other places? Well, we think the reason was obvious. There was idolatry in the land and they were commanded to destroy it. Since they did not destroy the idols they were commanded to gather in one place to worship. This unified the worship of the people and united them more as a nation. That unity was manifested when they would go up to Jerusalem to celebrate the feasts. It would also help them remember that there was only one God.

Nowadays it is not necessary for us to gather in one place to worship God. And the Lord Jesus Christ Himself gave the reason. You remember that when speaking to the Samaritan woman at the well, in John 4:21-24, Jesus said to her, *"Woman, believe me, the hour is coming when neither on this mountain nor in Jerusalem will you worship the Father. You worship what you do not know, we worship what we know, for salvation comes from the Jews. But the hour is coming, and now is, when the true worshipers will worship the Father in spirit and in truth, for the Father also seeks such worshipers to worship him. God is Spirit, and those who worship him must worship him in spirit and in truth".*

Therefore, today we do not gather in one place to worship God. However, there must be that "unity" of all believers, because we gather around one person and that person is the Lord Jesus Christ. That is the important thing to remember. The name of your church does not matter. The denomination or lack of denomination of your church does not matter either. When you gather with other brethren to worship, the most important question is do you gather around the person of Jesus Christ? Now, if not, then we are dealing with idolatry, because in this case, the worship gathering takes place around something or someone that is replacing Jesus Christ as the object of worship. What should spiritually unite the believers in unity is the person of the Lord Jesus Christ. How important that is! So let us begin this 12th chapter of Deuteronomy by reading the first four verses, in which it begins to be established,

One place to worship in the Promised Land

"These are the statutes and judgments which you shall observe to do in the land which the Lord, the God of your fathers, has given you to possess it, all the days that you live on the earth. You shall utterly destroy all the places where the nations which you shall inherit served their gods, on the high mountains, on the hills, and under every green tree. You shall tear down their altars, break their statues, burn their Asherah images, destroy the graven images of their gods, and erase their name from that place. You shall not do so to the Lord your God."

The reason why judgments descended upon Israel, one after another in the time of the judges, was because the people had fallen into idolatry. Then, that great prophet Elijah, directed his message against idolatry in that land. The reason why Israel suffered the Babylonian captivity was idolatry. And the warning in the last book of the Old Testament deals with the danger of idolatry.

We should not think that today we are exempt from the danger of idolatry. We have a tendency to believe that we are such cultured people, that we would never prostrate ourselves to worship an idol. But can we be so sure about that, dear listener? Anything that comes between our souls and God becomes an idol. How many people there are who, as they increase their commitment to their work or business responsibilities, and climb up the social ladder, progressively move away from God. This has nothing to do with their logical need to work and progress in their job, because in this competitive age, this is important. The problem is when work becomes an obsession that displaces spiritual priorities from the kingdom of God. In this case, a professional occupation has become an idol that has gotten in the way of a relationship with God. Let us now read verse 5, of this chapter 12 of Deuteronomy. And let us repeat verse 4:

"Ye shall not do so unto the Lord, your God, but the place which the Lord, your God, shall choose out of all your tribes, to put his name there, and to dwell therein, that shall ye seek, and thither shall ye go."

Eventually, the appointed place would be Jerusalem. But even before this, Israel was to worship in one place. There was to be a single place for their burnt offerings, other sacrifices, tithes and pledges. The tithes of food that they brought before the Lord had to be eaten in this place. Now, let us turn to verses 15 and 16:

"Yet you may slaughter and eat the meat in all your villages according to your desire, according to the blessing which the Lord your God has given you. Both the unclean and the clean may eat it, as if it were a gazelle or a deer. Only blood you shall not eat; you shall pour it out on the ground like water."

There was also the food they ate at home. This was not part of the worship, but it was also regulated by the dietary laws. In chapter 14 we will find an extensive list of clean and unclean animals. It was not necessary for a person to be ceremonially clean in order to eat at home. In addition to the animals that were reserved for sacrifice, they could eat game, as long as they were clean animals. The stipulation was that blood was not to be eaten. By contrast, anything that was an offering to the Lord had to be eaten before the Lord in one place, which would be appointed by God. Let us now turn to verse 21 and read to verse 25:

"If the place which the LORD your God chooses to put his name there is far from you, you may kill of the herds and of the flocks which the LORD has given you, as I have commanded you, and you may eat in your cities all that you wish. As the gazelle and the deer are eaten, so may you eat them; the unclean and the clean may eat of them. Only hold fast that you do not eat blood, for the blood is the life, and you shall not eat the life with the flesh. You shall not eat of it; you shall pour it out on the ground as if it were water. You shall not eat of it, that it may go well with you and your children after you, when you do what is right in the sight of the Lord."

In Leviticus chapter 17, while Israel was in the wilderness camp, they were commanded that whenever they killed a bull, or a lamb, or a goat, they were to bring it to the door of the tabernacle, and the priest would sprinkle the blood on the altar and offer the fat as a pleasing aroma to the Lord. This was intended to prevent them from making any offerings to the devils. Now, after settling in the land, it was obvious that very many would live too far from Jerusalem to bring every animal there before they killed it for food. Therefore, the Lord told them again that they could kill an animal for food, but they were not to eat the blood of that animal. The blood represented life. This is why Scripture places such emphasis on the blood of Jesus Christ. Let us turn now to verse 29 and read up to verse 31, Deuteronomy chapter 12:

"When the Lord thy God shall have destroyed before thee the nations which thou shalt possess, and thou shalt inherit them, and shalt dwell in their land, take heed lest thou stumble after their example, when they are destroyed before thee; and shalt not inquire after their gods, saying, How did those nations serve their gods, that I also should serve them after the same manner? Thou shalt not do so unto

the Lord thy God: for all the abominable things which the Lord abhorreth they did unto their gods: for even their sons and their daughters did they burn in the fire for their gods."

The Israelites were repeatedly commanded to destroy the nations that were in the land, lest they should be seduced by them. These nations were idolaters. Baal worship, like the worship of many pagan religions, had the very cruel practice of sacrificing their own children. They would heat an idol red-hot, and then drop their babies into the arms of that red-hot idol. We cannot think of anything more horrible than that! God said He abhorred such a practice. It was an abomination to Him. I realize that God abhors many things that I abhor too. I hope that I can learn more and more to abhor what He abhors and love what He loves. Let us read verse 32, which ends this 12th chapter of Deuteronomy:

"You shall take care to do all that I command you; you shall not add to it, nor take from it."

The Israelites, therefore, had to keep in mind these commandments that the Lord gave them. If they disobeyed God, God would treat them exactly as he treated the other nations. For God does not only observe the actions of some people and disregard the actions of others. Sin is sin, dear listener. And if Israel did not obey the Lord, they would not be forgiven. So the encouragement for them was to obey what the Lord commanded them to do.

And so we conclude this study of Deuteronomy chapter 12 and come to,

Deuteronomy 13:1-16

―――

N ow, chapter 13 is a very important chapter. The theme here is a warning about false prophets and how to examine false gods. When we get to Deuteronomy chapter 18, we will find the test for identifying false prophets. Israel had no problem detecting false prophets, because they had a biblical test given by God, which would surely uncover them. However, this chapter that we are examining today deals with the action to be taken against anyone who would try to lead the people away from their God, introducing false religions. Let us read then, the first four verses of this chapter 13 of Deuteronomy:

"When a prophet or dreamer of dreams arises in the midst of you and announces a sign or a wonder, if the sign or the wonder which he announced to you comes to pass, and he says to you, 'Let us go after other gods, which you do not know, and serve them,' you shall not listen to the words of such a prophet or dreamer of dreams, for the Lord your God is testing you to know whether you love the Lord your God with all your heart and with all your soul. The Lord, your God, you shall follow, and him you shall fear; his commandments you shall keep, and his voice you shall obey; him you shall serve, and him you shall be faithful."

This is pertinent for today. Many ask how we explain the fact that some of today's false prophets at times speak accurately. Or, they ask for explanations as to how it is possible that some seem to be healed at certain meetings. Well, we don't explain it. First of all, we believe that many of these cases probably have a natural explanation. But, even if there is something supernatural, God has warned that this can be accomplished through false prophets. And it is good to note this. When a false prophet performs supernatural signs, we should not believe in him if he denies the great truths of the Christian faith. That is the great principle of this passage, which we can apply. Now, notice what it says here in verse 5 of this 13th chapter of Deuteronomy:

> *"Such a prophet or dreamer of dreams shall die, because he counseled rebellion against the Lord, your God, who brought you out of the land of Egypt and redeemed you from the house of bondage, and sought to turn you from the way in which the Lord, your God, commanded you to walk. Thus shalt thou put away evil from the midst of thee".*

Let us note that any false prophet who tried to lead the people to some false cult or false religion was to be stoned. Now, does this measure seem extreme to you? Well, that false prophet was like a cancer and his destructive influence had to be neutralized. Here, God, as a great physician, said that this type of cancer should be removed from among the people.

This revealed the mind of God concerning the false prophets who were leading the people to false gods and false religion. And God gave these laws so that this would not happen in Israel. If anyone appeared in Israel trying to lead the people away from the worship of God, they were to kill that man. God understood how terrible it would be if they allowed false prophets to multiply. They would lead Israel into idolatry. And we must keep in mind that idolatry not only indicated a spiritual alienation from God, but also had implications that threatened the life and dignity of people, their health, the most basic human rights and the survival of children. Now, Israel did not obey God and allowed just that to happen. If you want to know how bad and harmful it was for God's people back then, read the story of Ahab and Jezebel, who led the nation into idolatry. This resulted in God's judgment on the Israelites, who were finally taken into captivity. Thus we see that the consequences were very serious. Now, let us read verses 6 through 9 of this 13th chapter of Deuteronomy:

"If you are incited by your brother, your mother's son, or your son, your daughter, your wife, or your intimate friend, saying to you in secret: Let us go and serve strange gods, which neither you nor your fathers knew, the gods of the peoples that are round about you, near you or far from you, from one end of the land to the other end of the land, you shall not consent to him nor give ear to him, your eye shall not pity him, you shall not have mercy on him nor cover him, but you shall kill him; your hand shall be lifted up first upon him to kill him, and then the hand of all the people."

Now, this was a concrete and extremely serious situation. It seems like a foreign language in an affluent and flexible society, such as this one in which we live. We know that this could not have been more severe but ultimately it saved many lives. When the northern kingdom went to idolatry what happened? Literally thousands of them were killed, and most of the survivors were taken into captivity as slaves, to the brutal nation of Assyria, where they were treated with extreme brutality. Now, in view of that fatal outcome, would it not have been much better if they had stoned the false prophets, those who led them into idolatry, first, instead of having a whole multitude killed and captured? Let us read verses 10 and 11:

"You shall stone him to death, because he sought to turn you away from the Lord, your God, who brought you out of the land of Egypt, out of the house of bondage, so that all Israel may know and fear, and never again do such a thing as this in your midst."

They were not to turn away from the living and true God. As long as they served Him, they would enjoy every blessing. But when they disobeyed Him, when they turned away from Him, punishment would come upon them. Judgments would descend upon them and that is their history. And that was the history of those people. Let us now read verses 12 to 14:

"If you hear that in any of the cities which the Lord your God gives you to live in, there have gone out from among your people wicked men who have instigated the inhabitants of their city, saying, 'Let us go and serve other gods, which you have not known,' you shall diligently investigate, seek and inquire. If it shall prove to be true that in the midst of you such an abomination has been committed."

They should not do anything rashly. A careful investigation was to be carried out in order to ascertain the truth before any action was taken. Let us continue with verses 15 and 16 of this chapter 13 of Deuteronomy:

"You shall surely smite the inhabitants of that city with the edge of the sword, destroying it and all that is in it, and you shall slay their livestock with the edge of the sword. You shall gather all its spoil together in the middle of the street and set fire to the city with all its spoil, all of it as a burnt offering to the Lord your God. It shall become a heap of ruins forever; it shall never be built again."

Evidently, this was also extremely severe, involving the destruction of an entire city. Cities were the center of expansion of pagan practices. As we said before, life and human dignity had no value in those societies that were self-destructing by such practices and by the contagion of contagious diseases, which were transmitted by the inexistence of sanitary controls, by the unbridled practice of sexuality and by the excesses of an uncontrolled diet. We cannot judge those rules from the perspective of our current society, in which diametrically opposed values on life and human rights, which have been embodied in advanced rules of social coexistence, still prevail.

We have mentioned on several occasions the death of those who with their pagan practices attempted against human life and dignity, in the times of the Old Testament. And as we conclude our segment, it would be good for us to remember that death entered the world because of sin, due to the wickedness of human beings. And in this topic we believe it is very significant to remember that Jesus Christ, the Son of God, was also tortured and led to death by the human beings of His time. He also suffered the innate violence of the human race. As the Evangelist Mark rightly said in 10:45, *He did not come into this world to exercise His authority over others, to be served, but to serve human beings and to give His life in payment for the freedom of many.* And then He rose again and today, whoever believes in Him and in His work on the cross, will have life after this life, that is, eternal life.

Deuteronomy 14:1-15:15

We said in our previous episode that the Israelites should not turn away from the living and true God. As long as they served Him, they would enjoy all kinds of blessings. But when they did not serve Him, when they turned away from Him, curses would come upon them. And judgments descended upon them and such punishments shaped their history. And so we conclude our study of Deuteronomy chapter 13. Now here in chapter 14, we find the diet for Israel. We studied already something about the diet for Israel, in the book of Leviticus 11 and the subject was mentioned again here in Deuteronomy chapter 12. The reason was that the dietary law that God had given them had already been tested during the march through the wilderness. First of all we note that

Pagan rites were prohibited

Let us then read the first two verses of this 14th chapter of Deuteronomy:

"Ye are the sons of the Lord your God: ye shall not cut yourselves, nor shave your heads for the sake of a dead man. For you are a holy people to the Lord, your God, and the Lord has chosen you to be to him a people unique among all the peoples that are on the earth."

These were pagan practices at that time. Today, we see the continuation of this custom in certain tribes that practice it. There are certain tribes in Australia that still disfigure their faces. It is part of their worship, of their religion. But God's people were never supposed to do such a thing. We now find,

Dietary laws

It would not be a bad idea if you went back to chapter 11 of the book of Leviticus, and read about clean and unclean animals. The diet God gave His people was more than just a religious ritual. There was actually a physical benefit to those who practiced it. This has been proven over the centuries.

There is a book about the plague that spread in Austria many years ago. The Jewish population did not suffer from the plague at all, while a high percentage of the rest of the population died. So, they blamed it on the Jews. Now of course, they had nothing to do with the plague. It was their dietary habits and living habits that protected them from the plague.

We live in a time when diets of all kinds are appearing. It seems that everyone is interested in them. God has not given us dietary laws that are specific to us. As far as our relationship with God is concerned, it does not matter whether we eat meat or not. However, God's dietary regulations were sensible and wholesome, and were conducive to health and survival. Let's continue reading here in Deuteronomy chapter 14 and read verses 3 through 6:

"You shall eat nothing abominable. These are the animals that you may eat: the ox, the sheep, the goat, the deer, the gazelle, the fallow deer, the ibex, the ibex, the antelope and the wild ram. You may also eat any animal with cloven hooves, that is to say, cloven in two halves, and which chews its cud.

There were clean animals that they could eat. And there were two characteristics that identified the clean animals and teach us some spiritual lessons.

The hoof of the animal had to be divided or split, separated into two claws. This detail speaks of the believer's walk. The separated hoof speaks of a separated life. It is not so much a life set apart from something, but a life set apart for something. The apostle Paul said in Romans 1:1, *that he had been "...set apart for the gospel of God".*

Now, we know that there is a legalism that has crept into the behavior of many Christians. There are people who do not limit themselves to living according to the Ten Commandments, but have added many others and try to live according to them. We do not believe that this is what God is indicating by means of the detail of the separate or separated hoof.

Now, the word for "cleave" actually has two opposite senses. To cleave can mean to disunite or split. Or it can mean to stick, cleave or cleave to something. This is also true of separation. One can be apart or separated from something, or apart, separated, for something. What is really important is not to set apart or separate oneself from certain activities or habits, but to set oneself apart for Christ. When one is separated for Christ, united to Him, the daily walk or conduct of the person will experience a radical change.

The second characteristic of the clean animals was rumination. The spiritual lesson here is that we should spend time with the Word of God. Psalm 1:2, speaking of the happy man, says: *"in the law of the Lord is his delight, and in his law he meditates day and night".* The first verse of this Psalm begins with the words, "Blessed is the man". The happy person delights in the law of the Lord and meditates on it. That word "meditates" has the sense of ruminating, which is illustrated by the cow, which has a complex stomach. The cow grazes in the morning when the grass is fresh and accumulates that grass in a compartment of her stomach. Later, when it is hot, it lies down under a tree or stays right there in the shade and transfers that grass from one section of its stomach to another, chewing it again. That is chewing. And that is what we should do with the Word of God, reading it and meditating on it.

Impure animals do not satisfy these two requirements. Some ruminate, but do not have a cloven hoof or two claws. The pig, for example, has a cloven hoof, but does not chew its cud. These animals were considered unclean and unfit to eat.

Some sea creatures were also considered unclean. Let us read verses 9 and 10:

"Of those that live in the water, these you may eat: everything that has fins and scales. But you shall not eat what does not have fins and scales; it shall be unclean to you."

In other words, they had to have two visible characteristics to be edible: fins and scales.

Then follows a list of the clean and unclean birds, in verses 12 through 16,

Tithing rules

Let us read verses 22 and 23 of this 14th chapter of Deuteronomy:

"You shall set aside a tenth of all the produce of the grain that your field yields each year. You shall eat before the Lord, your God, in the place which he chooses to put his name there, the tithe of your grain, of your wine and of your oil, and the firstlings of your herds and of your flocks, that you may learn to fear the Lord, your God, every day."

God had promised to bless His people in a material way if they would serve Him. Of that blessing they were to give a tithe or tenth part to the Lord, both of the fruit of the land and of their livestock. This tithe was to be eaten before the Lord, in the place of the sanctuary. This was to be a special feast before the Lord.

Now, if a family lived too far away (verse. 24 to 26) to bring their tithe of agricultural products or livestock, they could sell their tithe for money, to buy the equivalent of their tithe (such as, for example, oxen, sheep, wine) and the whole household was to eat it before the Lord. Now, according to verse 29, this tithe was to be shared during the feast with others. Let us read this verse, verse 29:

"There the Levite, who has no portion or inheritance with you, the stranger, the fatherless, and the widow who is in your towns, shall come there, and they shall eat and be satisfied, that the Lord your God may bless you in every work that your hands do."

And thus concludes our study of Deuteronomy chapter 14. We now turn to

Deuteronomy 15:1-15

———

In this chapter we find a double theme. First, the episode of God for the poor. And secondly, the permanent slave. Nowadays, we hear a lot of talk about assistance programs for the poor, many have been organized, but without success. God instead had an effective plan for the poor, which worked.

Then in this chapter there is a section on the permanent slave. And finally we find in this chapter 15, a figure of the perfect sacrifice, which is Christ. Let's begin by reading verse 1 of this chapter 15 of Deuteronomy, which begins to speak to us about the,

Sabbatical year

"Every seven years you shall make remission, that is, you shall forgive what others owe you."

Every seventh year was a sabbatical year. In that year they had to carry out a remission, a deliverance. Verse 2 says:

"In this is the remission: he shall forgive his debtor every one who has lent anything of his own, wherewith he bound his neighbor; he shall no longer demand it of his neighbor, or of his brother, because the remission of the Lord has been proclaimed."

God had already told them that every seventh year they were to leave the land fallow. The idea was to plow the land and leave it without sowing so that it would rest. And now we are told about the release of the seventh year. The Israelite could not take out a mortgage that lasted more than seven years. There could be no foreclosure. When the seventh year came, the money that had been borrowed or the mortgages that had been made, all had to be cancelled. This was a great compensating factor of wealth. It gave every man an equal opportunity.

All political systems today are confronted with the sinful, selfish nature of human beings. Therefore, theoretical formulations harmonize social inequalities and the provision of opportunities to people of any condition. But in real life, all systems give rise to situations of injustice that often produce social upheaval. God had a system for Israel that balanced opportunities so that the poor who really wanted to work would be able to make something of themselves. God's system avoided extreme wealth and extreme poverty. Let us now read verse 3 of this 15th chapter of Deuteronomy:

"From a foreigner you shall demand reimbursement; but what your brother has from you, you shall forgive him."

This regulation was to be observed by all Israelites. Every seventh year the debt of the poor would be cancelled and they would have a chance to start over again. Now, if Israel had kept this rule carefully, the next verse would have been applicable to them. Let us read verse 4 of this 15th chapter of Deuteronomy:

"So there will be no beggars among your people, for the Lord will bless you abundantly in the land which the Lord, your God, is giving you for an inheritance, to take possession of it."

Wherever one goes today, in whatever nation one visits, one is struck by the extremes of poverty and wealth. These extremes are the result of human sin. One can blame certain individuals, of course, but the root cause is man's sin. If the Israelites had obeyed God in this respect, there would be no poor among the members of that people, because the society would have been characterized by a balance of wealth.

It does not matter what system of government a nation has, or its political orientation. The fundamental problem will always be the human heart. As long as it is not transformed, the same old chronic problems will arise.

God called Israel to obedience. Had they obeyed Him, poverty would have been eliminated. It has already been duly demonstrated that poverty cannot be eradicated by funding charity programs. The result has been a spread of corruption at many levels. Why? The problem does not lie in a particular political system, nor in the programs created to solve the problems; the problem lies in the human being. Therefore, a change of system does not solve the situation. And we could pose a hypothetical case: What would happen if all the wealth of a nation were to be distributed equitably? Well, in a few years, because of selfishness and corruption, inequalities would reappear even more marked than before. Until the human being is changed, no system will work. And the problem is internal, in the human heart itself. If Israel had obeyed God, this problem would have been solved. But the Israelites failed. Why? Because of sin in their lives. Because of the sinful greed of human nature. Let us now read verse 6 of this 15th chapter of Deuteronomy:

"Since the Lord, your God, will have blessed you, as he has said to you, you shall then lend to many nations, but you shall not borrow; you shall have dominion over many nations, but over you they shall have no dominion."

Israel did not obey God, and therefore this prophecy has not been fulfilled. That is, it has been fulfilled only in part. Some Jews have become the bankers of the world. However, the nation of Israel has not obeyed God, and therefore the prophecy "you shall lend to many nations" has certainly been fulfilled, but the phrase "you shall have dominion over many nations but over you they shall have no dominion", has not yet been fulfilled. Let us now read verses 7 and 8:

"When there is a poor man among your brethren in any of your cities, in the land which the Lord, your God, gives you, you shall not harden your heart nor shut your hand from your poor brother, but you shall open your hand liberally to him and lend him what he indeed needs."

This is a very remarkable passage of Scripture. Israel never fully obeyed it when they were a nation, and they don't fully obey it today. But have you noticed something? Israel receives large donations from Jews all over the world. It probably receives more donations than any other nation.

It is that God taught them from the beginning that they were to take care of their brother. This same principle was also given to Christians. There are certain great fundamental principles, which are eternal truths, which God carries over from one age to another. This is what believers in Christ should be doing today. In the early church there was this solidarity among believers; but in reality, believers today, by and large, have not maintained this attitude of solidarity. And we are sure that even Israel did not do what God intended them to do when He gave them the instructions we have just read. Let us now read verse 9 of this 15th chapter of Deuteronomy:

"Beware of harboring in your heart this wicked thought: the seventh year is near, the year of remission, to look with evil eyes on your poor brother and give him nothing, for he might cry out against you to the Lord, and it would be counted to you as sin."

God warned them, saying that they should not look for a rational explanation to avoid their responsibility. They could say that, in any case, in the seventh year the brother would have no debt of any kind. Why, then, should they help him for a year or two? God commanded them to help the poor brother at that very moment. Let us now read verses 10 and 11:

*"You shall give to him without fail, and you shall not be
stingy-hearted when you give to him, for thereby the Lord your God
will bless you in all your works and in all that you undertake. For the
poor shall never be lacking in the midst of the land; therefore I
command you: You shall open your hand to your brother, to the poor
and needy in your land."*

God had told them that if they obeyed him, there would be no poverty on earth. But God knew them. God knows the human heart, and that is why He told them that they will always have the poor on earth. You will remember that the Lord Jesus said the same thing in Matthew 26:11. Jesus said, *"For ye shall always have the poor with you, but me ye shall not always have."*

Now, in verses 12 to 15, we are told about the slaves. And the slaves were to be freed in the seventh year. When the slave was freed, he was not to be sent away empty-handed. In our next episode we will continue with the subject of the permanent slave. But today, as we conclude, we ask ourselves a question and make a final reflection: What is the value of just and good norms, created to regulate social coexistence? No matter how much they are imposed by the public authorities, people always find ways to evade their personal and community responsibilities. There is no human power that can bend this tendency, this evil, this selfishness. Of course, reality can be disguised with a language of good intentions. And, of course, there are well-intentioned people who fight hard to remedy the injustices suffered by the less favored of this earth. But, when it comes down to it, only God can, by His Spirit, regenerate human beings. To this end, He sent Jesus Christ into this world to suffer for the sake of human sin, and to suffer the violence of men that would lead to His death. But Jesus conquered sin and death. And today He lives and is close to any person who invokes His name, to save them, to transform them, to free them.

Deuteronomy 15:16 - 17:20

We are nearing the end of Deuteronomy chapter 15. And in our previous episode, we were talking about "the sabbatical year", the year of remission. And we saw how every seven years, the Israelites were to make remission. And at the end we said that the slaves, they were also to be released in the seventh year. Now when the slave was released, he was not to be sent away empty-handed. Let us now look at the permanent slave. We have already made mention of the permanent slave when we studied Exodus chapter 21. Let us now read verses 16 and 17 of this 15th chapter of Deuteronomy:

"If he shall say unto thee, I will not leave thee; because he loveth thee and thy house, and because it is well with thee; then thou shalt take a lesna, and pierce his ear against the door, and he shall be thy servant for ever: so shalt thou do also unto thy handmaid."

We have already seen in Exodus chapter 21 that a man could sell himself into slavery. Now, if his master had given him a wife, that is, a woman who belonged, as a slave, to his master, when the sabbatical year came, the slave could go free. But, perhaps he would choose to keep the wife and children, and be a permanent slave of his master. Then, his master would pierce his ear with a lesna, signifying that he would be a slave forever. This is a beautiful description of the Lord Jesus Christ. Said the apostle Paul writing to the Philippians, chapter 2, verses 7 and 8: "He emptied himself, taking the form of a servant, being made in the likeness of men; and being found in fashion as a man, he humbled himself, and became obedient unto death, even the death of the cross." Jesus could have gone free. He had no sin debt to pay. He was not a sinner. He had no penalty to pay. But He loved us and gave Himself for us.

Just as the servant had his ear pierced with a lesna, the psalmist said in Psalm 40, verse 6: *"You have opened my ears"*. And the writer of the book to the Hebrews took the same passage from Psalm 40 and said in chapter 10 of that letter, verse 5: *"But thou hast prepared a body for me."* The Lord Jesus became incarnate, taking on a physical body so that He could be crucified for you and me. This is one of the most extraordinary descriptions we find of the Lord Jesus Christ in the entire Old Testament.

Verses 19 to 23 speak of the consecration of the firstborn males, and we already considered this matter when we studied Exodus chapter 13.

And so we conclude our study of Deuteronomy chapter 15.

Deuteronomy 16

In chapter 16, we find the 3 main feasts and the requirement was that all males must attend these feasts. We have already studied these feasts twice in the book of Exodus and also in the book of Leviticus. Let us read then, the first two verses of this chapter 16 of Deuteronomy, in which it begins to speak of,

Easter

"Thou shalt keep the month Abib, and keep a passover unto the LORD thy God: for in the month Abib the LORD thy God brought thee out of Egypt by night. And thou shalt sacrifice the passover unto the LORD thy God, of the flock and of the herd, in the place which the LORD shall choose, that his name may dwell there."

To understand the background of the Passover celebration, let us return to the book of Exodus, chapter 12. The children of Israel were in bondage in Egypt. Moses had been chosen by God to lead His people out of Egypt to the Promised Land. Pharaoh stubbornly refused to let them go, and God revealed His power to him by bringing plague after plague upon Egypt. On the terrible night, when the final plague was about to come, the children of Israel were to express their faith by sacrificing a lamb and marking the lintel of their door with its blood. Seeing the blood on the door, the angel of death would not enter the house and thus the life of the firstborn would be saved from death. Only upon the death of the firstborn in every house that did not bear the mark of blood, including that of his own son, did Pharaoh let the children of Israel go free.

God wanted His people to remember that great deliverance and thus instituted the great annual Feast of Passover.

Note that the Lord told them that when they entered the land, the Passover should be celebrated in the place of the sanctuary. This was one of the three times in the year when all the men were to appear before the Lord. Let us now read verses 5 to 8:

"Thou mayest not sacrifice the passover in any of the cities which the LORD thy God giveth thee; but in the place which the LORD thy God shall choose, that his name may dwell there, thou shalt sacrifice the passover in the evening at the going down of the sun, at the time that thou camest forth out of Egypt. And thou shalt roast it and eat it in the place which the LORD thy God shall choose: and in the morning thou shalt return and go unto thy habitation. Six days you shall eat unleavened bread, and on the seventh day it shall be a solemn feast to the LORD your God; you shall not work in it."

That was the regulation regarding the Passover. It was to be celebrated in Jerusalem, and all the males were to appear on that occasion. Let us now turn to consider,

The feast of Pentecost

Let us read verses 9 and 10 of this 16th chapter of Deuteronomy:

"Seven weeks shalt thou number: from the time that the sickle shall begin to be put into the harvest thou shalt begin to number the seven weeks. And thou shalt keep the solemn feast of weeks unto the LORD thy God: out of the voluntary bounty of thine hand shall be that which thou shalt give, according as the LORD thy God hath blessed thee."

Let us note that they had to count 7 weeks after the Passover, equivalent to 49 days. Then would come the Sabbath day, which would be the 50th day. Since the Greek word for 50 is "pentecost", the feast of weeks is known as Pentecost. It is also called "the feast of the harvest", or "of the first fruits". It was a celebration for the first fruits of the harvest.

Let us read verse 13 which begins to deal with the subject of,

The Feast of Tabernacles

"And thou shalt keep a feast of tabernacles seven days, when thou hast reaped the harvest of thy threshingfloor and of thy winepress.

This was another feast of rejoicing. It lasted seven days and was also to be celebrated in the place designated by the Lord. Later, that place was Jerusalem. Let us now read verses 16 and 17:

"Three times in the year shall every man of you appear before the LORD your God in the place which he shall choose: in the feast of unleavened bread, and in the feast of weeks, and in the feast of tabernacles. And no man shall stand before the LORD empty-handed, but every man with the offering of his hand, according to the blessing which the LORD thy God hath given thee".

These were the three feasts that were to be celebrated in Jerusalem, and to which every male was required to be present. Three times a year they were to travel to Jerusalem to celebrate these feasts with rejoicing. Let us observe that they were to come before the Lord with joy.

This chapter concludes with the commandments about judges. The next paragraph is entitled,

Judges at the gates

Let us now read verse 18 of this 16th chapter of Deuteronomy:

"Judges and officers shalt thou set in all thy cities which the LORD thy God shall give thee in thy tribes, which shall judge the people with righteous judgment."

The Palace of Justice at that time was not a building located in the center of town, not even in the main square. It was located at the edge of the city, at the gate of the wall built around the city. The reason for this was that this was a place where all the citizens entered or left the city. It was the meeting place, just as the square is the meeting place in many of our towns.

Knowing the human heart, as He knows it, God pronounced warnings about distorting justice, about favoring some people to the detriment of others and about bribes. Let us now turn to verse 21 and read verse 22 as well:

"Thou shalt not plant any tree for Asherah near the altar of the LORD thy God, which thou hast made thee, neither shalt thou set up unto thee any graven image, which the LORD thy God hateth."

A grove of trees was associated with idolatry and sinful worship at that time. And that is why trees were not to be planted near the altar of God. It was in those groves that the altars, images, and idols dedicated to the pagan gods were erected. It is easy to see that this is like the worship of the Druids in Europe. This was related to tree worship. Paganism had to do with that kind of thing, and God warned His people against that idolatry. And so concludes our study of Deuteronomy chapter 16.

Deuteronomy 17:1-19

―――

S ubject: capital punishment for idolatry and disobedience to authority. The laws about kings.

Now, in chapters 17 and 18 we come to a section that has to do with the regulations for the control of a king, a priest and a prophet. These were the three main offices in the nation of Israel, in the theocracy that God had established for His people. God dictated laws for each of these offices. Let us read then, the first verse of this chapter 17 that begins with the paragraph entitled,

The offerings were to be flawless

"Thou shalt not offer for sacrifice unto the LORD thy God, ox or lamb in which there is any blemish or any evil thing, for it is an abomination unto the LORD thy God."

G od had said that the firstborn of every creature belonged to Him. And that whatever was offered to Him as an offering should be without blemish and without defect. When we come to the last book of the Old Testament, we will notice that the prophet Malachi expressed the accusations that God brought against His people, and presented them as the reason for God's judgment upon them. God's main accusation was that sick animals were offered in the offering.

How honest are we in our financial dealings with God? Now, please don't misunderstand us. God is not poor. He is the owner of all the silver and gold. The thousands of animals on the hills are His. Figuratively speaking, He does not need our offering, some sick cow, or healthy cow. In reality, it is not possible for us to give God anything. So why does He ask for an offering? Well, He allows us to offer it to Him because it is a blessing to our own souls. We receive no blessing when we are poor and mean to God. God does not want our "leftovers" and leftover scraps He wants the best of us. Let us now read verses 2 through 5 of this 17th chapter of Deuteronomy which begins to deal with the subject of,

The death penalty for idolaters

"If there be found in the midst of thee, in any of thy gates, which the LORD thy God giveth thee, a man or woman that hath done evil in the sight of the LORD thy God in transgressing his covenant, and hath gone and served other gods, and bowed himself unto them, whether it be to the sun, or to the moon, or to all the host of heaven, which I have commanded not to be done; And it shall be told thee, and it shall come to pass, when thou hast heard, and hast searched diligently, that the thing seemeth sure, that such an abomination hath been done in Israel; then thou shalt bring forth the man or woman that hath done this evil thing, whether it be man or woman, unto thy gates, and stone them with stones, and they shall die.

This is a punctual law against idolatry. From this and other examples we deduce that the punishment for breaking any of the commandments was death.

Note that this passage mentions idolatry, which was common in the cultures of that time. Greek mythology and the idolatry of the East had many gods and goddesses who were related to the sun, the moon, and the stars. They honored and worshipped creatures before the Creator.

Now, what was the beginning of all this? Well, we believe it began at the tower of Babel. That tower of Babel was really a meeting place for all those who were against God. Why? God had sent a flood, and now they were going to worship the sun, because the sun, in their way of reasoning, would never send a flood. The most interesting thing was that they did not know that it is the sun that makes the water rise and moves the clouds across the sky, causing the rain to fall. The idolatry of that time was not very accurate, nor was their science. And perhaps the science of our times does not have the final word either. Many today believe that man's wisdom and knowledge are accurate. But, we know that in the past they have been inaccurate. They worshipped the sun, the moon and the stars, because they believed that the heavenly bodies favored them. They worshipped these, rather than the Creator, who made them. For this there would be condemnation from God for them. Let us now read verse 6, of this 17th chapter of Deuteronomy:

"He who is to die shall die by the testimony of two or three witnesses; he shall not die by the testimony of a single witness".

Let us observe how carefully God protected the innocent. His law would be just and not arbitrary. A man could not rush out of the city gates, and present himself to the authorities just because he disliked one of his neighbors and accuse him of worshipping the sun god, or Ashtoreth, the Babylonian god, or Baal, or Aphrodite, or any of the false gods. There had to be two witnesses, or more, to condemn the man. In some societies, a single witness can determine the condemnation of a person. This should not be so. God always required that there be two witnesses or more. God is very fair in His dealings.

We now come to a paragraph entitled,

Obedience to authority

Let us now read verses 8 and 9:

"When any thing shall be hard for thee in judgment, between one kind of murder and another, between one kind of legal right and another, and between one kind of wound and another, in matters of

litigation in thy cities; then shalt thou arise and go to the place which
the LORD thy God shall choose; and thou shalt come to the priests
the Levites, and to the judge that shall be in those days, and inquire;
and they shall teach thee the sentence of judgment."

In the theocracy they were to address their cases to the priest or judges, whom God would put over them. In a theocracy they should never have had a king. We know that later they asked for a king and God granted their request. Remember that Psalm 106, verse 15 says, *"And he gave them what they asked for; moreover he sent death upon them."* This was said in regard to their wilderness experience, but it is true for all times. If God were to answer many of our prayers, as we express them, it would be the biggest mistake in the world. God is gracious and often refuses to grant our requests. That is the way he acts with me and surely, with you as well. However, God would grant your request for a king. And here, before he even reached the promised land. He was setting standards for the king they would have in the future.

It was possible that the witnesses disagreed on an important issue. How was this problem to be resolved when the evidence appeared to be convincing on the part of both witnesses? Let us now read verses 10 and 11, of this 17th chapter of Deuteronomy:

"And thou shalt do according to the judgment which they of the place
which the LORD shall choose, and thou shalt observe to do according
to all that they shall show thee. According to the law which they shall
teach thee, and according to the judgment which they shall tell thee
thou shalt do; thou shalt not turn aside to the right hand nor to the
left from the sentence which they shall pronounce unto thee."

Since the law did not address all situations, disagreements were to be brought to the priest, and then they were to act in accordance with the decision given. Now, disobedience to the judgment of the priest was to be punished with the death penalty. Let us read here verse 12:

"And the man that dealeth proudly, not obeying the priest that standeth to minister there before the LORD thy God, or the judge, that man shall die; and thou shalt put away evil from the midst of Israel."

The only time we know that this procedure of consulting the priest was used is recorded in the book of the prophet Haggai, chapter 2, verse 11. But it says there in Haggai chapter 2, verses 11 and 12: *"Thus saith the LORD of hosts: Ask now the priests concerning the law, saying, If any man shall carry holy meat in the skirt of his garment, and with the flying of it touch bread, or meat, or wine, or oil, or any other meat, shall it be holy? And the priests answered and said, Nay".* Now, in case the law specifically dealt with a question and in a dogmatic way gave a regulation about it, then, obviously, there would be no need to take the matter to the priest, or to the judge. But if they had to take a matter to the priest, or to the judge, for him to make a decision, that decision, or verdict, was final, was binding, and had to be strictly obeyed. Let us see now,

The laws on the king

God knew that the time would come when they would want to have a king, just as the other nations had. Now, God said that their king should be an Israelite and not a foreigner. Let's read verses 16 through 19 of this 17th chapter of Deuteronomy:

"But he shall not increase horses for himself, neither shall he cause the people to return to Egypt for the purpose of increasing horses: for the LORD hath said unto you, Ye shall never return this way. Neither shall he take to himself many wives, lest his heart turn away; neither shall he heap to himself silver nor gold in abundance. And when he shall sit upon the throne of his kingdom, then shall he write for himself in a book a copy of this law, of the original which is in the keeping of the priests the Levites; and he shall have it with him, and

shall read therein all the days of his life, that he may learn to fear the Lord his God, to keep all the words of this law and these statutes, to do them."

Here we have the regulations for the king. It is interesting to note that King Solomon violated these regulations. First, he increased the number of horses. Solomon's stables would have made today's racetracks look small. This man, Solomon, made a supreme effort to increase his horses. And God admonished concerning this. To breed horses would make one entangled with Egypt, for that is where they bred the best horses. Then Solomon violated the second rule by taking to himself many women. God gave him warnings long before Israel had a king, not to act like that. However, Solomon took for himself many, many women. It was precisely his wives who turned him away from God, leading him into idolatry.

Third, God warned against heaping up for oneself silver and gold in abundance. However, that is exactly what Solomon did. David began to hoard silver and gold, but David was doing it for the building of the temple. Regardless, Solomon continued to hoard the silver and gold for himself. This was the ruin of Solomon and the onerous taxation was the direct reason for the division of the kingdom into northern and southern kingdoms after Solomon's death.

Let us finally read verses 18-20

Now, finally, the king was to be a man of the Word of God. He was to have a particular copy of God's law and he was to read it every day of his life.

We would like to conclude, as we began, by recalling that slave with the pierced ear. We said it was a beautiful description of the Lord Jesus Christ, who out of love renounced what was his own and assumed the nature of a servant, living among us, until he suffered death on the cross. you and I, and all other human beings, have all been the object of that love. How will you respond to it?

Deuteronomy 18:1 - 19:21

We continue our study in the book of Deuteronomy and come to chapter 18. This chapter deals with the priests and prophets, and the test to recognize the true prophet. God gave laws about the financial support of the priests. Then there was another admonition against idolatrous practices, which had recourse to satanic powers. This is followed by one of the outstanding sections of this book of Deuteronomy. It has to do with the prophets, and there is a wonderful prophecy concerning the Lord Jesus, the Prophet who was to come. The section on the prophets concludes with an interesting and important test to distinguish between false and true prophets. Let us first look at the "inheritance of the priests". Let us read the first two verses of this 18th chapter of Deuteronomy, in the paragraph entitled:

The care of priests

"The Levitical priests, that is, the whole tribe of Levi, shall have no part nor inheritance in Israel; of the burnt offerings of the LORD and of his inheritance shall they eat. Therefore they shall have no inheritance among their brethren; the LORD is their inheritance, as he hath said unto them."

The priests were of the tribe of Levi. All the Levites were helpers in the temple and in worship. They had no inheritance among the children of Israel. Their inheritance was not a portion of land, but the Lord himself was their inheritance. The Lord provided for them in a unique way. It was interesting that God did not mention how a king would get his wages, but gave instructions on how a priest would get his. Let's continue with verses 3 to 5:

"And this shall be the right of the priests from among the people, of them that offer the bullock or the lamb for sacrifice: they shall give to the priest the shoulder, and the cheeks, and the rind. The first fruits of thy corn, of thy wine, and of thine oil, and the first of the wool of thy flock, shalt thou give him: for the LORD thy God hath chosen him out of all thy tribes, to be a steward in the name of the LORD, he and his sons for ever."

Here we have a great principle that God established. We believe that this is still the method God uses to carry out His work in the world. We believe that God expects His people to financially support the work of proclaiming the Word of God to the world. Let us now look at the prohibition of the,

Spiritism

Let us read verses 9 through 12 of this 18th chapter of Deuteronomy:

"When you enter the land which the LORD your God is giving you, you shall not learn to do according to the abominations of those nations. Let no one be found in you who makes his son or his daughter to pass through the fire, or who practices divination, or a fortune-teller, or a sorcerer, or a wizard, or an enchanter, or a charmer, or a soothsayer, or a magician, or one who consults the dead. For it is an abomination to the LORD whoever does these things, and for these abominations the LORD your God drives out these nations from before you."

When the Israelites entered the Promised Land, they were not to follow the pagan customs practiced by the inhabitants of that land. The apostle Paul warned in his first letter to Timothy, chapter 4, verse 1, that: "...in the last times some shall depart from the faith, giving heed to seducing spirits and doctrines of devils". That is to say, they will be taking hold of that unseen and satanic world.

Now, let us speculate, and you can believe as you see fit. But we believe that we have now reached that period. There are churches of Satan, where they actually worship Satan. Many say this is nothing more than a novelty. They say it is a tendency of human nature to follow whatever is new. But we believe that there is a lot of reality in the worship of Satan. It is not a group of ignorant people, nor of little cultural preparation. There must be a reality, since Satan is real, and we believe that those who participate in this do find a real experience in this worship. And God warned about this.

We want to say this because it is necessary today, that someone says it. There is a danger of playing with astrology. Remember that in the previous chapter we read the condemnation of the worship of the sun, the moon, and the stars. And there are many people who put more emphasis on astrology than on the Bible. The magazine stores are full of material on this subject. We see it everywhere.

This kind of thing is an abomination to the Lord, for it leads many away from the living and true God. It plunges them into darkness and belief in demons. There is a reality about the demon world. There are fallen angels and the spirit world. It is a reality and people are intrigued by it. They use drugs and they use every means possible to try to communicate with that unseen world, the satanic world. And that world is very, very happy to communicate with them.

A child of God should not get involved in these things. Anyone who takes a step in that direction reveals that he has a weak faith and does not truly trust Christ as his personal Savior. That means you are turning away from the true Holy Spirit and the Word of God. God has given warnings concerning this kind of thing. His warnings have been very accurate in the past, so we had better follow and obey Him! Let us now look at verses 13 and 14 of this 18th chapter of Deuteronomy:

"Thou shalt be perfect before the LORD thy God. For these nations, which thou shalt inherit, shall hear the prophets of doomsayers and soothsayers; but the LORD thy God hath not permitted this unto thee."

Those nations in the promised land were to be judged for this very cause. Israel had been called to be a witness of the living and true God. Let us continue with verses 15 through 17, which begin the paragraph entitled,

The promise of a prophet

"A prophet from among you, of your brethren, like me, will the LORD your God raise you up; him shall you hear; according to all that you asked of the LORD your God in Horeb in the day of the assembly, saying, Let me not hear again the voice of the LORD my God, neither let me see this great fire any more, that I die no more."

The children of Israel were to listen to the prophets. Why? Because they spoke the truth. That was the fundamental thing. But the second reason they should listen to their prophets was because they were being prepared to listen to the final Messenger, the final Prophet, the Lord Jesus Christ.

Some still ask why God does not reveal Himself today. In the person of the Lord Jesus Christ, God brought the sentence to a close. God wrote the "finished" at the end of the book. God put the last quotation marks to the quotation. He had nothing more to say to the world than what had been said in Jesus Christ. We must listen to Him. We must pay attention to Him. You will recall that at the transfiguration, which took place on a mountaintop, God the Father said in Matthew 17:5 *"This is my beloved Son, in whom I am well pleased; hear ye him."* He is the final word.

For believers today, the Lord Jesus Christ is the final, complete and ultimate revelation of God to man. This is what Moses was saying here in the book of Deuteronomy. Let us now read verses 18 and 19:

> *"A prophet will I raise up for them from among their brethren, like you; and I will put my words in his mouth, and he shall speak to them all that I shall command him. But whosoever will not hear my words which he shall speak in my name, I will call him to account."*

The Lord Jesus Christ said over and over again that the words He spoke were not His own, but the Father's. He said that the words He spoke were not His own, but the Father's. For example, in chapter 14 of the Gospel according to John, verse 10, He said that the words He spoke were not from Himself, but from the Father. In chapter 5, verse 30 of the Gospel of John, and many times in chapter 6, the Lord Jesus said that He did not come to do His own will, but to do the will of the Father. And when the Lord finished His earthly ministry, He prayed in that great priestly prayer, in which He gave His final report to the Father, in John chapter 17, saying, *"I have finished the work which thou gavest Me to do."* He had spoken all that the Father wanted Him to say.....

If God were to speak from heaven at this very moment, He would not say anything that has not already been said by Him. He would simply repeat Himself. Everything He is trying to say to you and me is found in the person of Christ.

That is why we should not get involved in astrology. It is the tendency of human nature to want to explore the unknown, to know about the future. There is an insatiable desire to explore the mysterious. There is something of that spirit of Christopher Columbus in all of us. Right now we are exploring space and the depths of the oceans. We like to expand knowledge into new areas. We do this not only in space, but also in time. Man wants to know something about that mysterious future. Memory can take us back to the past, but there is no similar vehicle to take us into the future, on whose door there seems to be a sign saying "No Entry". It is evident that the human being has great limitations in terms of time and space.

In order to satisfy this insatiable craving, men such as spiritists and magicians arose among the heathen, as well as methods of divination. God warned His people about these things, because they were related to idolatry and were satanic in origin. Could they foretell the future? Well, there was some degree of accuracy. The Greeks made use of the oracle at Delphi and apparently they received some accurate information there. But that was satanic. Some say that Hitler, for example, went to some kind of soothsayer. And the advertisement section of some newspapers in our cities will reveal to you that there are many fortune tellers who make their living by talking about the future. Many of their predictions are so general that they must necessarily be accurate for some. But let us remember that man has never been given any control over the future.

Only God can predict the future. It belongs to Him. That is the unique character of God's Word. It reaches beyond the present. The greatest proof to me that the Bible is the Word of God is the fulfillment of prophecy. One-fourth of the entire Bible was prophecy at the time it was written, and a large portion of that prophecy has already been fulfilled. God has recorded prophecies concerning cities and nations and great world empires. Under such circumstances, false prophets would arise, just as they have arisen today. They want to have the legal status and position that belonged to the true prophet of God. How could the Israelites protect themselves from false prophets? God gave a test by which they could be sure whether a man was a true prophet of God, or a false prophet.

So let's see,

The test for distinguishing between true and false prophets

It was evident that there were false prophets among the people. Unfortunately, Israel would not apply God's rules to identify them. We read in Jeremiah chapter 14, verse 14, and you had better look it up too, *"Then the Lord said unto me, The prophets prophesy falsely in my name: I sent them not, neither commanded them, neither spake I unto them: they prophesy unto you a lying vision, divination, vanity, and deceit of their heart."* As you see, it was easy for the false prophets to speak of coming kingdoms and future centuries. The prophet Jeremiah also spoke of the future. Now, how could one tell who was the true prophet? Today we can know because a large part of Jeremiah's prophecy has already been fulfilled. But how was it possible for the Israelites to know at the time the prophecy was spoken? Well, God gave them a test that would give an accurate result. Returning to Deuteronomy chapter 18, let's read verses 20 to 22:

"The prophet who presumes to speak a word in my name, whom I have not commanded to speak, or who speaks in the name of other gods, that prophet shall die. And if thou shalt say in thine heart, How shall we know the word which the LORD hath not spoken? if the prophet speak in the name of the LORD, and it come not to pass, neither come to pass, it is a word which the LORD hath not spoken: with presumption hath that prophet spoken it; be not afraid of him."

Let's consider this for a moment. Isaiah was a prophet of God, a true prophet of God. Now, how do we know this? He prophesied that the virgin would conceive and bear a son. He clearly pointed to the coming of the Lord Jesus; His birth, His life and His death. Now, suppose some had asked Isaiah, when was all this going to take place? He would have replied that he was not quite sure, but that it might take place after hundreds of years. (Actually it was 700 years). Well, that group would laugh and say that by that time, they wouldn't even be around to know if he had told the truth, or not. The test would be that all true prophets would have to give predictions as to local situations that were to occur immediately, and they would have to be rigorously accurate. They could not err in any detail of their prophecy. Any inaccuracy would instantly disqualify them as true prophets of God.

Now, let's look once again at Isaiah. He prophesied the virgin birth and today we can look back 2000 years to the fulfillment of that prophecy and know that it was accurate. But how could the people of that time know that? Well, they could know because Isaiah went to King Hezekiah with a prophecy about an event of his time and told him not to be afraid. There was an Assyrian army of about three hundred thousand bow-hungry soldiers surrounding the city, but Isaiah said that not a single arrow would enter the city. These Assyrians had conquered other nations and were there to conquer Jerusalem, and to take Israel into captivity. But Isaiah told Hezekiah what God had said about them, and we can read it in Isaiah 37:33 and 34, which says: *Therefore thus saith the LORD concerning the king of Assyria; He shall not come into this city, nor shoot an arrow into it; he shall not come before it with a shield, nor set up a bulwark against it. By the way that he came, he shall return, and shall not come into this city, saith the Lord.*

All these soldiers of the Assyrian army had bows and arrows. It was to be expected that one of them would let fly an arrow over the wall, simply to see if he could hit someone. It was to be expected that in an army of three hundred thousand men, there would be a soldier eager to shoot the arrow. Now, if even one arrow entered the city, Isaiah lost his position as a true prophet of God. But do you know that not one arrow entered the city? Not even one. So Isaiah passed the test with his prophecy. There were other times when Isaiah spoke about a local situation, and it happened just as he had said. The true prophet had to get it right all the times he prophesied.

Now, what shall we say about our time? This test would disqualify anyone who claims to be a prophet predicting the future. A true prophet must be accurate in every detail, whenever he speaks about the future. But did you know that there is no warning, today, concerning false prophets for the Church? And do you know why not? Because there is no more prophecy to be revealed. All has already been revealed in the Lord Jesus Christ and in His Word. The warning that concerns us today is not about false prophets, but about false teachers. The apostle Peter spoke of this in his second letter, chapter 2, verse 1, when he said: *"But there were also false prophets among the people, just as there will be false teachers among you".* The advice to us is to listen very carefully to the teaching of God's Word. Whatever we are told today, it must be according to the Word of God. Everyone can study the Word of God. That is our criterion. But we must beware of false teachers, and we must judge what they say according to their conformity or lack of conformity to the Word of God.

And so concludes our study of Deuteronomy chapter 18 and we come to,

Deuteronomy 19:1-21

N ow in chapter 19 we are told about the cities of refuge, the extent of the land and the severity of the law. This chapter 19 begins with instructions as to,

Cities of refuge

I n the book of Numbers 35, we saw that the Levites had to establish 3 of these cities on the eastern side of the Jordan, and 3 on the western side.

By way of summary of verses 2 to 4, we will say that a man who had accidentally killed another, could flee to a city of refuge. This did not apply to premeditated murder. God clarified that these cities of refuge would provide protection for the innocent and gave an example of what he meant by accidental death. In verses 5 and 6 he said that two men were working together on the mountain. As their hand struck the blow with the axe to cut down some wood, if the iron on the headland jumped and killed one of the men, the other was allowed to flee to the city of refuge, where he would be protected from the angry reaction of some relative of the dead man or from the wrath of the crowd, until he could be fairly tried. The Lord specified that these cities would not be to protect those who were guilty of premeditated murder...Let us then look at what related to the extent of the land. Let us read verses 8 and 9 of this 19th chapter of Deuteronomy:

"And if the LORD thy God shall enlarge thy coast, as he sware unto thy fathers, and give thee all the land which he promised to give unto thy fathers, if thou shalt keep all these commandments which I command thee this day, to do them; that thou mayest love the

LORD thy God, and walk in his ways all the days; then thou shalt add three more cities unto these three."

The test of love is obedience. If Israel had obeyed God, the Israelites would have been blessed and God would have extended their land. Then they could have added three more cities of refuge. But they never needed them for the simple reason that they only occupied part of the promised land. Now, let us read verse 14 of this 19th chapter of Deuteronomy, which tells us about,

Protection of property rights

"In the inheritance which thou shalt possess in the land which the LORD thy God giveth thee, thou shalt not diminish the bounds of thy neighbor's property, which the ancients fixed."

We have here the fact that the boundaries were inviolable. This was the protection of human property, and establishes property rights. Let us read verse 15 of this 19th chapter of Deuteronomy, to consider,

The severity of the law

"Not a single witness shall be taken into account against any one in any crime nor in any sin, in relation to any offense committed. Only by the testimony of two or three witnesses shall the indictment stand."

This passage reveals to us how terrible the law was. The demands of the law were tremendous, and one witness was not enough in any case. Anyone who says today that he wants to live under the law should find out what the law really entails.

Now, in verses 16 through 20, the Lord explained if a false witness was raised, then the accused and the accuser were to stand before the Lord, represented by the priests and the judges. Now, if the judges decided that the witness was false, then what he wanted them to do to the accused would be precisely the punishment he himself would receive. Thus the wickedness was to be removed from the nation. Let us now read verse 21, the final verse of this 19th chapter of Deuteronomy:

"And you shall not pity him; life for life, eye for eye, tooth for tooth, hand for hand, foot for foot."

That is the law, dear hearer. There was nothing of mercy in the law. I am thankful that the Lord today, is not judging me on the basis of the law. He saves me by grace. If He saved me by the law, I would be lost forever, because it would never be possible for me to meet the requirements of the law. The law is the law. At the present time we have adopted a very indifferent attitude towards it. But God executed the law, and surely we remember the phrase "An eye for an eye, a tooth for a tooth." How I thank God that Jesus Christ paid the penalty of the law, so that there would be forgiveness for sinners! The judgment seat of Christ has become a place of mercy because Christ died and His blood has been sprinkled there, as of old, on the mercy seat or lid of the ark, and that was the blood of the New Covenant. God saves us by His grace. We have not kept the law; we have broken it. We are all guilty before God. But Christ paid the penalty so that the requirements of the law could be fulfilled. Now, God is free to save sinners, by His marvelous and infinite grace. That is why He saved me, and He can save you too.

Deuteronomy 20:1 - 21:23

———

C ontinuing our tour through the book of Deuteronomy, we come to chapter 20. In this chapter we find the laws about war. This book of Deuteronomy is a very practical book. It refers to life as we live it today. Although this law was given to Israel, there are certain basic principles here that would contribute to the happiness and well-being of mankind, if they were incorporated into our daily lives.

The problem today is that we live in a society that does not know the Bible. In the vast majority of countries, many legislators do not know much about the Word of God, or if they do, they would not see fit to impose principles not accepted by a secularized society. This book of Deuteronomy addresses problems, which political leaders have struggled to analyze and solve in their own way.

Israel had problems similar to those of today. God gave certain very basic regulations that would excuse a man from going to war. Frankly, we believe that if our governments would pay more attention to God's law, we would not have to face the difficulties we face and which do not seem to have a solution.

So let's see,

The laws of war

L et us read the first verse of this 20th chapter of Deuteronomy:
"When you go out to war against your enemies, if you see horses and chariots, and a people greater than you, do not be afraid of them, for the LORD your God is with you, who brought you out of the land of Egypt."

Here is something that was of great importance to Israel, and we believe it is important to us today. You may have seen those little signs that proclaim: "Love yes! War no!". Now, that seems like a nice slogan, but like so many other slogans, it's meaningless. Because we live in a world where evil predominates and the human heart is wicked, there are times when there is no choice but to engage in armed conflict. There are times when we need to protect ourselves.

Let us continue reading verses 2 through 4 of this chapter 20:

> *"And when ye draw near to fight, the priest shall stand and speak unto the people, and shall say unto them, Hear, O Israel, ye are gathered together this day to battle against your enemies: let not your heart fail you, neither be ye afraid, nor be dismayed, neither be ye dismayed at their presence: for the LORD your God goeth with you, to fight for you against your enemies, to save you."*

Here we see that in that particular situation God commanded them to make war against these nations and promised to be with them. Now, let us read verse 5:

> *"And the officers shall speak unto the people, saying, Who hath built a new house, and hath not begun it? Let him go and return to his house, lest he die in battle and another build it.*

Now God gave four conditions under which a man would be exempt from going out to battle. If a man had built a new house and had not yet had the opportunity to live in it, he did not have to participate in a battle. Why? Because his heart would be in that new house. He had put his heart and affection into it. He wanted to live in that new house and he had to have the opportunity to live in it. Now, let's read verse 6:

> *"And who has planted a vineyard, and has not enjoyed it? Go, and return to your house, lest you die in battle, and some one else enjoy it."*

The Israelites were husbandmen, and the planting of a vineyard was their work or occupation. If a man had just planted a vineyard and had not yet had the opportunity to eat a grape from his vineyard, he need not go to battle. His heart was set there, in that vineyard; his interest is there. He could then stay until he had eaten from it, until he had established himself as a farmer. Otherwise, he ran the risk of being killed in battle, and another would reap the fruit of his labor. Now verse 7:

"And who hath espoused a wife, and hath not taken her? Go, and return to his house, lest he die in the battle, and some one else take her."

Here we have a man who was engaged to marry a woman, and even if he was drafted, he didn't have to go into battle. He was in love with that young woman, and he wanted to marry her. He could stay home, and marry his bride. That's where his heart was, and he didn't have to go off to war. Now verse 8, gives us the 4th excuse:

"And the officers shall return and speak to the people, and say, Who is a man of a stubborn and fainthearted spirit? Go, and return to your house, and do not grieve the heart of your brethren, as your own heart."

There could be a man who would frankly admit that he was a coward. He was afraid to fight. He wanted to stay at home. We see here, then, four good reasons why a man was exempted from going to war.

This law was applied to Gideon's army. Gideon started with a few men, actually there were 32,000 who joined him to rid his country of the oppression of the Midianites. But the Lord told him that they were too many soldiers, and for those who were afraid to return home. When this disposition spread, 22,000 soldiers remained. Then the Lord told Gideon that he still had too many soldiers. But how to reduce the number? They came to a brook and some of the men knelt down to drink. There were others who licked the water with their tongues, as a dog licks, and were soon ready to fight. They were very anxious to defeat the enemy and finish their work. They wanted to protect and save the nation. Therefore, in the end there were only 300 left and they were the ones who went out to battle. The others were sent home.

And so ends our study of Deuteronomy chapter 20. We now come to chapter 21. In this chapter 21 we find the laws regulating murder, marriage, and delinquent children. We are still in the section dealing with religious and national regulations, which extends from chapter 8 to 21. We find that there are interesting and extraordinary laws, which ruled on many different aspects of Israel's life. Let us look at them first,

The laws regarding murder

Let us read the first 4 verses of this 21st chapter of Deuteronomy:

"If in the land which the LORD thy God giveth thee to possess it, a man be found dead, lying in the field, and it be not known who slew him; then thy elders and thy judges shall go out, and measure the distance unto the cities which are round about the dead man. And the elders of the city nearest to the place where the slain man is found shall take a heifer that has not been worked, that has not been yoked; and the elders of that city shall bring the heifer into a rough valley, which has not been plowed or sown, and shall break the neck of the heifer there in the valley".

If a man had been murdered and his body was found, they had to measure the distance to find the nearest city to the place where the body was found. That city was considered responsible for the murder. Now, he may not have been murdered in that city, but still, the city was responsible. Now let's see what he had to do. Let's read verses 5 through 9 of this 21st chapter of Deuteronomy:

"Then shall the priests the sons of Levi come, for them hath the LORD thy God chosen to minister unto him, and to bless in the name of the LORD: and by their word shall all disputes and all offences be decided. And all the elders of the city nearest to the place where the slain man was found shall wash their hands over the heifer whose neck was broken in the valley; and they shall protest and say, Our hands have not shed this blood, neither have our eyes seen it. Forgive thy people Israel, whom thou hast redeemed, O LORD; and lay not innocent blood upon thy people Israel. And their blood shall be forgiven them. And thou shalt take away the guilt of innocent blood from the midst of thee, when thou shalt do that which is right in the sight of the LORD."

There is a fundamental truth that we are taught in this procedure. When a crime took place in a city, the inhabitants of that city bore some responsibility. God held a community responsible. Even if the murder was not committed in the city, the city was still responsible. The elders of that city were to come and ask forgiveness for the city, and forgiveness would be granted. God so arranged it so that there could be no shirking of that responsibility in Israel.

In the New Testament we will see that Christ was killed outside the city. He was. And it was His death that was able to save His murderers. We believe that the Roman centurion, the one who was in charge of the execution of His death sentence, was one of the men who were saved by believing in Jesus Christ.

Now verses 10 through 17 give laws regulating marriage to a wife imprisoned in war, and laws dictating the legal protection of the rights of the firstborn, in the case of a man who had two wives, and loved one and hated the other. We have seen this situation in the life of the patriarch Jacob.

Let us now look at the laws concerning,

Delinquent children

Let us read verses 18 through 21 of this 21st chapter of Deuteronomy:

"If any man have a stubborn and rebellious son, which will not obey the voice of his father, nor the voice of his mother, and when they have chastised him, he will not obey them; then shall his father and his mother take him, and bring him out before the elders of his city, and to the gate of the place where he dwelleth; and they shall say unto the elders of the city, This our son is stubborn and rebellious, he obeyeth not our voice; he is a glutton, and a drunkard. Then all the men of his city shall stone him with stones, and he shall die: so shalt thou put away the evil from the midst of thee, and all Israel shall hear, and fear."

We have here a law concerning the prodigal son. Let us recall the parable of the "prodigal son" that we saw in the Gospel according to Luke, chapter 15. This is what should have happened when the prodigal son returned home. We can then understand how our Lord Jesus Christ impacted the crowd listening to him, when he told them the parable of the prodigal son. The crowd believed that the boy would be stoned. We can imagine their surprise when Jesus Christ said "the father went out to meet the boy". They were expecting the young man to receive what he justly deserved. This boy was due dishonor. He deserved to die. But what did the father do? He embraces the son and said, "My son was lost, and has been found."

Dear, I am glad that we are not under the law today. When we come to God and confess our sins, "He is faithful and just to forgive us our sins and to cleanse us from all unrighteousness." Instead of judgment, there is mercy for us. Instead of judgment, there is mercy for us. How wonderful and merciful God is, accepting and receiving us when we come to Him! Let us now read verses 22 and 23, of this 21st chapter of Deuteronomy:

"If a man has committed a crime worthy of death, and you put him to death and hang him on a tree, you shall not let his body remain on the tree all night; you shall bury him the same day without fail, for he who is hanged is accursed of God; and you shall not defile your land which the Lord your God is giving you for an inheritance."

A criminal who was executed by hanging on a tree, i.e. crucified, was not to be left on the cross all night. That was because all those hung on a tree were cursed by God. Now, it seems strange to us that this law was mentioned here. The form of capital punishment that was used in Israel was stoning. Apparently, the Israelites did not use crucifixion as a form of capital punishment. What this means then is that they stoned a person to death, and then hung him on a tree. Verse 22 says here: *"...and you shall put him to death and hang him on a tree".* This was applied to criminals of the worst kind, so that everyone could see that he had died for his terrible crime and to serve as a lesson to others. The body was removed from the tree at nightfall and was to be buried. Now, the reason for this was that the criminal had been cursed by God.

We believe that neither Moses nor the children of Israel realized the full meaning of this law. The apostle Paul, writing his letter to the Galatians, chapter 3, verse 13, spoke concerning this statement in the reading and applied it to Christ. He said, *"Christ hath redeemed us from the curse of the law, being made a curse for us (for it is written, Cursed is every one that hangeth on a tree)".*

In our Lord's time, He was delivered into the hands of the Romans for execution. Since they ruled in Palestine, the death penalty could only be carried out by Rome. Our Lord was crucified on a Roman cross. Rome handed over the decision to crucify Him, and He was put on a tree.

Now, Paul highlighted that fact and said that when Christ hung there on the tree, he took our sins and in that condition he was cursed of God. He became a curse for us because He redeemed us from the curse of the law. He redeemed us from the curse of sin. He redeemed us from the penalty of sin, and has purchased our forgiveness. Why? Because he was made a curse for us.

Disputes about whether the Romans or the Jews are to blame for the death of the Lord Jesus are unimportant. Actually, you and I were guilty of His death. He took upon Himself the curse of the law for us, that we might be redeemed from the curse of the law. He redeemed us from the curse of the law once and forever.

Have you noticed how many times the book of Deuteronomy is quoted in the New Testament? A book like Deuteronomy is very important. It would be difficult to understand much of the New Testament without having an understanding of the book of Deuteronomy.

Deuteronomy 22:1 - 23:7

—————

We continue our study today in the book of Deuteronomy and come to chapter 22. In this chapter we find miscellaneous laws regarding sibling relationships, clothing, building codes, agriculture and marriage. We now come to another division of the book of Deuteronomy. This book gives a repetition of the law from chapters 5 to 26. First, we have the repetition and interpretation of the Ten Commandments in chapters 5 to 7. Then we find the religious and national regulations, from chapter 8 to chapter 21. And now, we come to the regulations regarding domestic and personal relationships, which are found in chapter 22 to chapter 26. And now we come to the regulations which are very practical, and which have to do with domestic and personal relationships. Let us look then, first of all, at the relationships between brethren. Let us read the first two verses of this chapter 22 of Deuteronomy:

"If you see your brother's ox or his lamb gone astray, you shall not withhold your help from him; you shall bring it back to your brother. And if thy brother be not thy neighbor, or thou knowest him not, then thou shalt bring him into thy house, and he shall be with thee until thy brother seek him, and thou shalt restore him to him."

In our times we have heard a lot about the good neighbor policy. God had His good neighbor policy for His people back then. You may remember that during President Franklin D. Roosevelt's administration in the United States, he came out with the good neighbor policy. And all the scholars and reporters applauded it and said this was brand new. They hailed Roosevelt as if he was some kind of Messiah and they thought he had come up with something wonderful. let us tell you that the good neighbor policy is as old as

Moses himself and much older than Moses. It dates back to the very throne of God in eternity. He is the one who says that we must adopt the good neighbor policy. This must be demonstrated in our daily living. Let us now continue with verse 4:

"If you see your brother's donkey, or his ox, fallen on the road, you shall not turn away from him; you shall help him to lift it up."

They should not assume an attitude of indifference toward their neighbor. Nor should they act as if the neighbor's problem was of no concern to them. They should extend their help to their neighbor. Now, let us look at some laws related to clothing. Let us continue with verse 5 of this chapter 22 of Deuteronomy:

"A woman shall not wear a man's garment, neither shall a man put on a woman's garment: for every one that doeth this is an abomination unto the LORD thy God."

Someone will say that this does not apply to us today, because we are not under the law. That is true. However, all these laws that we are studying, give us certain principles that we do very well to look at. We believe it is still true today, that a woman looks much better dressed as a woman, and a man looks better dressed as what he is, as a man.

God created us male and female. And God is saying here, that a man should look like a man and a woman should look like a woman. We have a lot of difficulties today, because the sexes try to look alike and try to behave alike. We believe that it costs the female sex dearly for that. They demand equal rights. And we believe that they have had more than their equal rights. Men like to treat women like women, and that means that men like to exalt them. We believe, personally, that women really lose by demanding equal rights.

Let us now look at some laws related to the protection of birds. Let us read verses 6 and 7 of this chapter 22 of Deuteronomy:

"When you find by the way any bird's nest in any tree, or on the ground, with chickens or eggs, and the mother lying on the chickens or on the eggs, you shall not take the mother with the children. Thou shalt let the mother go, and take the chickens for thyself, that it may be well with thee, and thou mayest prolong thy days."

God is interested in birds. Remember that the Lord Jesus said there in the gospel according to Matthew, chapter 10, verse 29, that not even one little bird falls to the ground without the Father knowing about it. Actually, the language there in that portion of Scripture, has the sense that a little bird always falls into the bosom of the Father. Just a little bird! Yet the Father has an interest in him. And the Lord goes on to say in Matthew 10:31: *"Fear ye not therefore: ye are of more value than many sparrows."* How wonderful that is! If the Father has an interest in a little bird, He also has an interest in you and knows all about you.

Let us now consider what we might call the building code. Let us read verse 8 of this 22nd chapter of Deuteronomy:

"When thou buildest a new house, thou shalt make a parapet on thy housetop, lest thou bring blood upon thy house, if any man fall therefrom".

It is necessary to understand that the roof of the house at that time in Israel was like the porch facing the street. It was the place where the family went out to sit in the cool of the evening. Now, God says that the roof should be protected. There was to be a railing around the roof, so that the little ones would not fall, and so that people would not fall off the roof in the dark.

Do you know that it is only in these last few years that we have building codes to protect people? God is not as old-fashioned as many believe him to be. God has an interest in the way men build their homes. Yes,

He has an interest in that. He wants your house to be dedicated to Him, and He wants that house to be a safe place.

Here's another thought: Do you have a railing around your house? Do you protect your children from the things of this world? How many parents let their children go out without knowing where they are going? How many children have gone out to live in bad company that corrupts their good habits? Still today, we need to have those guardrails around our homes.

Let us now look at the sowing of the seed. Let us read verse 9 of this chapter 22 of Deuteronomy:

"Thou shalt not sow thy vineyard with divers seeds, lest all be lost, both the seed which thou hast sown and the fruit of the vineyard."

As you see the seeds were not to be mixed. And God goes on to give more laws regarding the mixing of things. Let's look at verse 10:

"Thou shalt not plow with ox and ass together."

Now this seems like a funny thing that the Lord says here. But the truth is that it is so in Israel, even today. You can see an Arab in the field plowing with an ox and an ass together. Well, God says that Israel is not to plow that way. Maybe somebody says, "Well, what's wrong with that? An ox is an ox. And an ass is an ass. And they don't go together. They don't walk together, they don't work together. They are not alike and should not be put together.

Now, have you noticed that the Lord did not like any hodgepodge? The same is true in marriage. God does not want any mixture between the saved and the unsaved. Unfortunately, we have seen many, many marriages where an ox and an ass have come together. That is what happens. Now, let's read verse 11 of this chapter 22:

"Thou shalt not wear wool and linen together."

Do you know what happens with a combination like that? When you wash it, the wool will shrink, but the linen will not shrink. It results then in a real problem. Now verse 12:

"Thou shalt make thee bangs on the four ends of thy cloak with which thou coverest thyself."

Those bangs were usually blue in color. There was a blue color on the high priest's garment. The fringe was at the edge of the garment where it touched the earth. The heavenly blue was to touch the earth. There is a lesson in this for the child of God. God admonishes concerning mingling. The child of God cannot mingle with the world. There are some Christians who mix with those of the world, under the pretext of being able to reach them. But beware. That is not the way to reach them. If you hear that someone has been reached because a Christian has consorted with those of the world, please let me know. The seed was not to be mixed. The ox and the ass were not to work together. Wool and linen were not to be combined in a garment. And in the same way, the Christian should not mix with the world.

Let us now consider some laws related to marriage. Let us read verses 13 through 15 of this chapter 22 of Deuteronomy:

"If a man shall take a wife, and after he has gone in to her shall hate her, and shall lay upon her faults that make one speak, and shall say, I took this woman, and went in to her, and found her not a virgin; then the father of the damsel and her mother shall take and bring forth the tokens of the maiden's virginity to the elders of the city, in the gate."

We have here a law to protect the innocent wife, and it was to prevent a wife from being falsely accused. This law protected a wife from an unfaithful, ungodly, and hateful husband. God had made an arrangement to protect a wife under such circumstances. And you see what happened to the husband who had raised that false accusation. Let's read verses 18 and 19:

"Then the elders of the city shall take the man and punish him; and they shall fine him a hundred pieces of silver, which they shall give to the father of the damsel, because he has spread an evil report about a virgin of Israel; and he shall keep her to wife, and shall not be able to put her away all his days."

Now, what happened if the accusation was true. Let us continue reading verses 20 and 21:

"But if it shall prove true that virginity was not found in the damsel, then they shall bring her out to the door of her father's house, and the men of her city shall stone her with stones, and she shall die, because she hath wrought wickedness in Israel by playing the harlot in her father's house: so shalt thou put away the evil from the midst of thee."

If the woman was guilty, she was to be stoned to death. Today men talk about the new morality, and they think it is a great step forward. But God gave a standard of morality to His people Israel. And the morality given by God has always served as a blessing to any nation. Any nation that has violated God's law of morality has fallen. And when we think about this, and when we think about the condition of our countries, it really makes us want to weep.

Under God's law for Israel, a person guilty of adultery was stoned to death, whether male or female. If we did this in our countries, there might be nowhere to build roads. There would be so many stone piles everywhere that, well, it would be impossible to open roads.

The rest of this chapter continues to deal with this same subject. God honors marriage, and God honors sexual purity. Adultery in Israel was to be punished by death. Death by stoning.

And so we conclude our study of this chapter 22 of Deuteronomy. And the central theme of this chapter is: the world, the flesh and the devil. We live in a time when men speak very frankly. The fact is that sometimes the language becomes vulgar. There are some passages that we do not read publicly. However, in these passages there are some great spiritual lessons that we should not miss.

We have entitled this chapter: "The World, the Flesh, and the Devil". We believe that we deal daily. And in fact every hour and every moment, with these three enemies. Let's look at the first verse of this 23rd chapter of Deuteronomy:

"He shall not enter into the congregation of the Lord whose testicles are bruised, or whose manhood is amputated."

This is a very strange law, don't you think? What is God trying to teach here? This would correspond to asceticism, and God condemns it.

During the Middle Ages men saw depravity in Europe, in Asia, and in North Africa, and they turned away from the things of the world, and became ascetics. They entered monasteries to withdraw from the world. And this is an extreme against which God warns.

It is possible to find the same type of legalism today, in Protestantism. There are people who believe that they live the separate life. Many things are denied. However, we have not found these people to be joyful. The fact is that some of them are very dangerous. They behave in a very pious manner and seem to be shocked when anything that is worldly is mentioned in front of them. But we have found that these same people can be the most gossipy. Sometimes they are not honest in their business dealings. We have found that those who appear to be the most out-of-the-way are the most untruthful. God warns against asceticism. Such an individual will not enter the congregation of the Lord. Let us now read verse 2:

> *"A bastard shall not enter into the congregation of the LORD; neither shall they enter into the congregation of the LORD until the tenth generation."*

God uses frank language here. An illegitimate child could not enter the congregation of the Lord. Now, what does that mean for us today?

It means that you have to be reborn to become a child of God. There are many today, who say they are children of the King. But in reality they are not children of the King. They are illegitimate. One can be religious without being reborn. And such an individual is not a child of God, in any way. And God expresses this very clearly. Nicodemus for example was a Pharisee, a very religious man, a spiritual leader of the people, someone who wore his phylacteries. However, that man was illegitimate, and our Lord told him that it was necessary for him to be born again. Our Lord interrupted him in an almost impolite way to tell him there in the gospel of John, chapter 3, verse 3: *"...Verily, verily, I say unto thee, Except a man be born again, he cannot see the kingdom of God".*

A pastor once said: "There are many pagans today who are baptized. They are sinners bound for hell and they believe that because they have been baptized, they are children of God". God says that the illegitimate child will not enter the congregation. God has no illegitimate children. All His children are legitimate, because they have been reborn. And let us ask you this question: Have you been reborn? Do you know Christ as your personal Savior?

The Gospel of John in chapter 1, verses 12 and 13, says: *"But as many as received him, to them gave he power to become the sons of God, even to them that believe on his name: which were born, not of blood, nor of the will of the flesh, nor of the will of man, but of God" (John 1:12-13).*

Do you meet the requirements to be a legitimate child of God? It does not matter how many ceremonies you have performed, or how many churches you have attended, or how religious you are. Unless you are a child of the King, you are illegitimate. Let us continue reading verses 3 and 4 of this 23rd chapter of Deuteronomy:

"Neither shall Ammonite nor Moabite enter into the congregation of the LORD, even to the tenth generation of them; they shall not enter into the congregation of the LORD for ever, because they met you not with bread and water on the way, when ye came out of Egypt, and because they hired against thee Balaam the son of Beor, of Pethor in Mesopotamia, to curse thee."

Archaeologists have discovered that the Ammonites and Moabites were the worst pagans. They have discovered many of their images to Baal. And this speaks of false religion. False religion must not enter the congregation of the Lord. Now, how is it possible for one to recognize false religion? The Lord says there in Matthew 7:16: *"By their fruits ye shall know them"*. The evidence was that they would give Israel neither bread nor water, and they hired Balaam to curse Israel. Let us continue now with verses 5 and 6 of this 23rd chapter of Deuteronomy:

"But the LORD thy God would not hearken unto Balaam; and the LORD thy God turned the curse into a blessing unto thee, because the LORD thy God loved thee. Thou shalt not seek their peace nor their good all the days for ever."

We realize that this seems to be a terribly harsh thing to say, but this is a terrible admonition against any liaison with false religions. False religion is satanic in origin. And the devil must not enter the congregation of the Lord. It is false religion that has condemned this world to eternal damnation, more than anything else. It is possible that a very beautiful church, with a high tower, and sweet music to the ear, may be the very house of Satan. We must therefore be on our guard against false religion. False religion has no place in the congregation of the Lord. Let us now read verse 7 of this 23rd chapter of Deuteronomy:

"You shall not hate the Edomite, because he is your brother; you shall not hate the Egyptian, because you were a stranger in his land."

We saw in the book of Genesis that Edom represents the flesh. Edom is Esau, and Esau and Jacob were twin brothers. Now, they were to hate the Ammonites and the Moabites, but not the Edomites, that is, the flesh.

You and I have an old nature, the flesh. We may well abhor the flesh, try to step on it, try to punish it, but none of that does any good. We must not abhor the flesh, nor must we mutilate it. On the other hand, that old nature must not control us, and we must not yield to the flesh. The flesh is still in rebellion against God. However, it is a part of us. And to abhor it is of no avail.

Now, they were not to abhor an Egyptian. Egypt always represents the world. They had been strangers in the land of Egypt. And we are pilgrims in this world. It is true that we should not love the world, but neither should we abhor the world. The Puritans were extremists. They tried to deny everything in the world. The world is still our home here, even if we just pass through it. If we could always remember that we are pilgrims here in the world, we would have the world in its proper perspective.

Let us say that the children of Israel were never commanded to plant flowers in the wilderness. They were called to go through it. That is our calling today. We are to pass through this world, but we are not commanded to associate with movements whose purpose is to set the world to rights. Nor are we to compromise with the world. What we are to do is to give the world the Word of God. That is what we are trying to do here in this episode "Through the Bible".

So, as you see, in a way this chapter is about our relationship with the devil, who motivates false religions, and it is also about our relationship with the flesh and with the world. And the Christian cannot agree with any of the three.

Deuteronomy 23:10 - 25:16

T oday we continue our study of Deuteronomy chapter 23. And we are going to consider some various regulations. Let's read verse 10 of this chapter 23:

"If there be in the midst of you any man that is not clean by reason of any uncleanness by night, he shall go forth without the camp, and shall not enter therein."

God tells them here that they must have a clean camp, and gives them some regulations regarding sanitation. God has an interest in sanitation. Wherever Christianity has entered, there has been an improvement in sanitary conditions.

We hear a lot of talk today about pollution. Now, who polluted this universe? God certainly did not pollute it. He gave us the clean streams, the clean air, the clean water. It is sin, the sinner, that pollutes this earth today. If men would follow the regulations God has given, this earth would be a healthy place. Let us turn now to verse 14 of this 23rd chapter of Deuteronomy:

"For the LORD thy God walketh in the midst of thy camp, to deliver thee, and to deliver thine enemies before thee: therefore let thy camp be holy, lest he see any unclean thing in thee, and turn away from following thee."

God is interested in cleanliness. We believe it was Webster, who said that cleanliness is the next best thing to holiness. And we believe that cleanliness is a part of holiness. We must be clean of body, clean of environment, clean of mind, clean of thought, and clean of action. We must be a holy people in the world today. This book is very practical, don't you think? Now, let's turn to verse 17 and let's also read verse 18 of this 23rd chapter of Deuteronomy:

"There shall be no harlot among the daughters of Israel, nor shall there be a sodomite among the sons of Israel. You shall not bring the wages of an harlot or the price of a dog into the house of the LORD your God for any vow; for both the one and the other is an abomination to the LORD your God."

God did not want harlots and sodomites among His people. However, it seems that the people disobeyed God and there were some in that land. God says that He will not accept money from that which is unlawful or immoral, because He does not want any of it.

Now, let's say something, here we know it's not going to bring us much popularity. We believe that no Christian organization should receive money from any industry that is illegal or immoral. We know that the liquor industries for example try to make donations to charitable organizations, as a cloak to cover their clandestine activities. But we believe, and repeat that no Christian organization should accept such donations. Let us now read verses 19 and 20:

"From thy brother thou shalt not exact interest for money, nor interest for foodstuffs, nor for any thing whereof interest is customary. From a stranger thou mayest require interest, but from thy brother thou shalt not require it, that the LORD thy God may bless thee in all the work of thy hands in the land whither thou goest to possess it."

We have here a regulation regarding their business dealings and borrowing money. Let us continue with verses 21 and 22:

"When thou vowest a vow unto the LORD thy God, delay not to pay it; for the LORD thy God will surely require it of thee, and it would

be sin in thee. But when you abstain from vowing, there shall be no sin in you."

A vow to the Lord was a voluntary thing. No one was required to make a vow. However, once a person had made a vow to the Lord, that vow was categorically obligatory. We have already discussed this above. Now verses 24 and 25:

"When you go into your neighbor's vineyard, you may eat grapes to your heart's content, but you shall not put them in your basket. When you go into your neighbor's harvest, you may pluck the ears of corn with your hand, but you shall not put a sickle to your neighbor's harvest".

We saw in our study of chapter 12 of the Gospel according to Matthew, that the disciples of our Lord Jesus Christ, did just this. They were hungry and so they began to pluck ears of corn and eat. Now, this was not unlawful. God had ordained this method in order that the poor might eat.

And thus concludes our study of this 23rd chapter of Deuteronomy. We come now to chapter 24. And in this chapter 24, we will deal with "divorce". We find here the Mosaic law concerning divorce. Now, why was Moses allowed to give this kind of law about divorce? Our Lord explains it clearly. You remember back in Matthew chapter 19, verses 7 to 9, they said to him, "Why then did Moses command to give a bill of divorcement, and to put her away? And he said unto them, Because of the hardness of your hearts Moses suffered your wives to put away: but at the beginning it was not so. And I say unto you, Whosoever shall put away his wife, except it be for fornication, and shall marry another, committeth adultery: and whosoever shall marry her that is divorced committeth adultery".

Let us then look at the Mosaic law of divorce. Let us read the first 4 verses of this chapter 24 of Deuteronomy:

"When a man shall take a wife, and marry her, if she please him not, because he hath found in her any thing unseemly, then he shall write her a bill of divorcement, and deliver it into her hand, and send her out of his house. And when she has left his house, she may go and marry another man. But if the latter hate her, and write her a bill of divorcement, and deliver it into her hand, and send her away from his house; or if the last man that took her to wife be dead, her first husband that sent her away may not take her again to wife, after she is defiled: for it is an abomination before the LORD, and thou shalt not pervert the land which the LORD thy God giveth thee to inherit.

This seems like a pretty easy way to divorce, doesn't it? And so it was. For if the wife let the biscuits burn, the man thought that was reason enough to give her a bill of divorce. And this was not God's intention, as we read clearly from the words of Jesus. The law was given because of the hardness of their hearts. You will notice that after a divorce, the ex-husband could not take a wife again. God does not agree with wife-swapping. There should be no change from one to another. Our Lord gave only one basis for divorce and that was unfaithfulness in marriage.

There is some speculation as to the passage in the apostle Paul's first letter to the Corinthians, chapter 7 and we will talk about that when we get there in our study. We don't want to get into that topic now, but it probably uncovers another motive or basis for divorce. Jesus said that Moses had been permitted to give this law, because of their hardness of heart. There are many, many things that God sanctions in His permissive will. He permits them because of the hardness of our hearts. And this is still true today in many cases of divorce. It is also true in many of our homes and in the personal lives of many individuals.

God has been merciful and gracious to us. But let's understand one thing and that is that it is not according to His direct will. It is according to His permissive will. And He manifests His grace to us. Knowing this, it behooves the more spiritual brethren not to criticize others so much today. Let us now read verse 5 of this 24th chapter of Deuteronomy:

"When a man is newly married, he shall not go out to war, nor shall he be occupied in anything; he shall be free in his house for a year, to make his wife happy, whom he has taken."

God protects the home even in time of war. God respects the sanctity of the marriage vow.

And we turn now to consider some miscellaneous regulations also here in this 24th chapter of Deuteronomy. Let us read verse 7:

"When a man is found to have stolen from one of his brethren the children of Israel, and to have enslaved him, or sold him, that thief shall die, and thou shalt put away the evil from among you."

We see here that God condemns slavery. There is no doubt about that. Let us turn now to verse 20 and read up to verse 22 of this 24th chapter of Deuteronomy:

"When thou shalt shake thine olive trees, thou shalt not go over the boughs which thou hast left behind thee: they shall be for the stranger, for the fatherless, and for the widow. When thou gatherest in thy vineyard, thou shalt not glean after thee; it shall be for the stranger, for the fatherless, and for the widow. And remember that you were a servant in the land of Egypt; therefore I command you to do this."

God was taking care of the helpless, those less fortunate. God had a good plan for the poor, and the interesting thing is that it was successful. We will see this a little later, when we come to our study of the book of Ruth.

And so we conclude our study of Deuteronomy chapter 24. The central theme of this chapter 25 is the "Punishment of the guilty; the law that protects widows; the punishment for crimes committed and the judgment of Amalek". We are still in the section of this book of Deuteronomy that gives a repetition of the law. This subdivision has to do with the regulations of domestic and personal relationships.

Let us look, then, first of all, at "the punishment of the guilty". There were certain crimes that arose because of difficulties between individuals. We believe that in our legal nomenclature today, we would call them misdemeanors. These were not serious crimes that merited the death sentence. However, they did require punishment. So let us read the first three verses of this 25th chapter of Deuteronomy:

"If there be a controversy between some, and they come to the judgment seat to be judged by the judges, the judges shall acquit the righteous, and condemn the guilty. And if the offender deserves to be scourged, then the judge shall cause him to be cast to the ground, and shall cause him to be scourged before him; according to his offence shall be the number of stripes. Forty stripes may be given, but no more; lest, if he be beaten with many stripes more than these, thy brother be disgraced in thine eyes".

They could not give more than forty lashes. Otherwise, there was danger of killing the man. We suppose that they actually used any number of lashes during their very long history. But the number of lashes, one to 40, depended on the seriousness of the crime. This is a method of punishment that has gone completely out of fashion. But there are lawyers today who believe that much of our present-day debauchery could be stopped if there were public flogging. When a man is arrested for a crime, he is usually put in an air-conditioned jail so he can loaf around. Now, he doesn't mind loafing, so he is not really being punished. But if he were taken outside and publicly flogged, he would not be so willing to commit the same or more offenses. God thought that whipping would stop a lot of crimes, and so he arranged it that way. And we do not believe that there were many crimes in Israel. We doubt that the level of crimes in Israel would reach the level of crimes in our countries today. Let us now read verse 4 of this 25th chapter of Deuteronomy:

"Thou shalt not muzzle the ox when he thresheth."

We see here a kind thing. God protects the ox. However, you can see there some of those oxen today, going round after round threshing, and muzzled. God had said they should not muzzle him. The ox is working; he is threshing. And God says he has a right to eat.

Now, the apostle Paul refers to the book of Deuteronomy and uses this verse in his first letter to the Corinthians, chapter 9, verses 9 to 11 when he says: "For it is written in the law of Moses, Thou shalt not muzzle the ox that treadeth out the corn. Does God care for the oxen, or does he say it entirely for our sakes? For it was written for us: for he that ploweth ought to plow in hope, and he that thresheth in hope to receive of the fruit. If we sow among you spiritual things, is it a great thing if we shall reap from you material things?"

Do you see how the apostle Paul applies this? He says: "Pay the preacher!" The man who feeds you with spiritual things is feeding you spiritual food. You in turn, must feed him with material food. This is how Paul makes the application of this verse.

As I sit here and talk to you, I make a recording. And I watch the hands of the clock go round and round and round. I feel like the ox that is threshing. And you know? That's what I'm trying to do for you: thresh.

God forbid we should muzzle the threshing ox. So I'm going to let you make your own application of this.

We now move on to another point. We believe that God has a sense of humor. God has a law here, concerning the care of widows. It was effective, as we will see in the book of Ruth. But, to us, it seems a little funny. So let's read verses 5 and 6 of this 25th chapter of Deuteronomy:

"If brethren dwell together, and one of them die, and have no child, the wife of the dead man shall not marry without unto a stranger: her brother in law shall come unto her, and take her to him to wife, and be unto her a kinsman. And the firstborn which she shall bear shall succeed to the name of his dead brother, that his name be not blotted out of Israel".

God protected the female sex. We hear a lot of talk today about feminism. And it is interesting that God protected their rights. We must remember that in Israel, the majority of the people were farmers. The land was divided among the people, and each one had his own portion of land. Now, when a man died, he left a farm with all his wheat and corn, and also his flocks of sheep and oxen. The widow was left with this farm to take care of. Let us suppose then that some man from outside, some foreigner or man from another tribe wanted to marry her, and thus obtain possession of the land. She could not do that, because that was forbidden. She was not allowed to marry an outsider. We have here a case in which the widow is the one who declares herself. What she had to do was to go and demand that one of her husband's brothers marry her. If she had no brother, she would go to the cousin. And so she was to go to the nearest kinsman and propose, asking him to marry her. Let us now continue with verses 7 through 10 of this 25th chapter of Deuteronomy:

"And if the man will not take his sister-in-law, then his sister-in-law shall go to the gate to the elders, and say, My brother-in-law will not

raise up a name for his brother in Israel; he will not be related to me. Then shall the elders of that city bring him in, and speak unto him: and it shall come to pass, if he stand up, and say, I will not take it; then shall his sister in law come near unto him before the elders, and take off his shoe from off his foot, and spit in his face, and speak, and say, So shall it be done unto the man that will not build his brother's house. And this name shall be given him in Israel, The house of the barefooted."

If the man refused to marry her, the woman could then take him to court. The city gate was the court in those days, and the wife could take him to the elders and explain her case. Now, if he refused to marry the widow, there was a penalty. He was disgraced for not doing what he was supposed to do according to the law. It revealed the fact that he had not been faithful to his brother, nor to his family, nor to his tribe, nor to his nation, nor to his God. The man was dishonored.

We have here a wonderful example of the way God protected the widow. We will see the validity of this law when we come to the book of Ruth. It was used effectively in that book.

Can you imagine how this would affect a family in Israel? Suppose there was a family of four children, living on a farm in the country of Ephraim. Now, suppose that night after night one of the boys would go out with the lantern or lantern, or torch, and when he came to bed, he would always come in whistling and singing. Soon the family would gather and the brothers would ask him where he was going night after night. They would also inquire until they discovered that there was a daughter in the family who lived down the road. So, the brother would confess that he believed in the good neighbor policy and had gone there to visit her. And, he would have to confess that he was thinking of marrying the girl.

Now, if those brothers did not like the girl, can you imagine what would happen? They would say, "Look, before you think about marrying that girl, go to the doctor and have her examine you. We want to make sure that you are in good health before you marry her, because none of us want to take care of her. This was serious business, my listening friend. Getting married was a family affair. So it is easy to see how this brought the family together. This was God's method of bringing the family together in a closer relationship, and also to protect the widows and the land. For in this way, the land would always remain in the family. This then, was a very good law.

Verses 11 through 16 of this 25th chapter of Deuteronomy name certain crimes that are committed when men quarrel. Men were also commanded to be exact in their weights and measures.

Deuteronomy 25:17 - 28:15

———

I n Exodus 17 we have the account of Amalek's attack on the Israelites, when they left Egypt. And they attacked them once again when they reached Kadesh-barnea. The Amalekites were nomads in that wilderness. Let us first read verses 17 to 19 of this 25th chapter of Deuteronomy:

"Remember what Amalek did with thee in the way, when thou camest out of Egypt; how he met thee in the way, and smote thee in the rear of all the feeble ones that followed thee, when thou wast weary and weary; and he had no fear of God. Therefore, when the LORD thy God shall give thee rest from all thine enemies round about, in the land which the LORD thy God giveth thee for an inheritance to possess it, thou shalt blot out the remembrance of Amalek from under heaven; forget it not."

Israel had been attacked by Amalek at Rephidim. That was the battle in which Moses stood on the top of the hill, and Aaron and Hur held up their arms in prayer to God. When Moses raised his hand, Joshua and the army of Israel triumphed. But when he lowered his hand, Amalek prevailed. They finally won a victory over Amalek. At that time God said something very interesting. "I will utterly blot out the memory of Amalek from under heaven."

We have already mentioned that Amalek represents the flawed physical nature we have inherited from Adam. And God intends to get rid of that nature controlled by the passions. The old nature cannot enter heaven. You and I have an old nature that can never be obedient to God. No doubt you know that you have that old nature that can never be obedient to God. We will deal with this matter further, when we come to the Apostle Paul's letter to the Romans. But Amalek is an illustration of such a fallen nature. While we are in this life, we will never be done with it.

The Lord also made the following statement. We read in Exodus 17:16: *"...and he said, Because the hand of Amalek is risen up against the throne of the Lord, the Lord will have war with Amalek from generation to generation".* We saw already in the previous chapter that we must not despise the old nature. We cannot overcome it by being ascetics, or by trying to bring it down, or by being religious or pious. That would accomplish nothing. What we need is to recognize that there is a struggle going on in each of us. It is a struggle between the Spirit and the physical nature. The apostle Paul said writing to the Galatians 5:17: *"For the evil desires are against the Spirit, and the Spirit is against the evil desires; the one is against the other, and therefore you cannot do what you would."* We cannot overcome this nature by struggle. The only way we can overcome it is by submitting to the Spirit of God. Only the Spirit of God can produce the fruits or results of the Spirit's work in our lives. The Lord says that He would blot out the memory of Amalek from under heaven. And we thank God that someday, He intends to do away with that old nature someday, symbolically represented by Amalek.

And so we end our consideration of Deuteronomy chapter 25. We turn now to,

Deuteronomy 26

In this chapter 26, we find **"the first fruits of the land and thanksgiving".** Recognizing that all the produce of the land came from God and as an expression of their thanksgiving for the divine goodness, the Israelites brought him a portion of the fruits that ripened first, as an offering to God. Let us read the first four verses of this 26th chapter of Deuteronomy:

"When thou shalt come into the land which the LORD thy God giveth thee for an inheritance, and shalt possess it, and dwell therein, then thou shalt take of the firstfruits of all the fruits which thou shalt bring forth out of the land which the LORD thy God giveth thee, and shalt put them in a basket, and shalt go unto the place which the LORD thy God shall choose, to cause his name to dwell there. And thou shalt go unto the priest that shall be in those days, and say unto him, I declare this day unto the LORD thy God, that I am come into the land which the LORD sware unto our fathers to give us. And the priest shall take the basket from your hand, and set it before the altar of the LORD your God.

In presenting his offering of the first fruits to the Lord, Moses reviewed the history of God's action on behalf of the people in delivering them from oppression in Egypt and leading them to the Promised Land. Let us read verse 5:

"Then you shall speak and say before the LORD your God, 'An Aramean about to perish was my father, who went down to Egypt and dwelt there with few men, and there he grew up and became a great nation, strong and numerous'"

Let us note a detail here. Moses first approached God with an attitude of confession. The Israelite would confess his identity by saying: An Aramean about to perish was my father. What was Abraham's nationality? Was he an Israelite? No. He was not really an Israelite. And Isaac? Well, he wasn't an Israelite either. And Jacob? Technically, Jacob was not an Israelite. (He was the one whose name would be changed to Israel). Well, all of the group that went down to Egypt were Syrians. (They came out of the other side of the river. That's why they were called Hebrews. Hebrews means they came from the other side). Abraham was therefore a Syrian or Aramean by nationality, as it says here. He was no more an Israelite than an Ishmaelite, since both peoples descended from him. He was the father of many nations. (Moses could therefore say that his father was Syrian, or Aramean as the verse says. One family; only a few, went down to Egypt. And there they became a great nation). After Moses told them their story, he told them that when the Lord brought them into the promised land, then they should make an offering to God. Now, verse 10:

"And now, behold, I have brought the firstfruits of the fruit of the land which thou gavest me, O LORD. And thou shalt leave it before the LORD thy God, and worship before the LORD thy God."

For the Israelite it would thus be a time to express his gratitude to God. Now, the second part of the chapter deals with the declaration of obedience to God. Let us read verses 12 and 13:

"When thou hast made an end of tithing all the tithe of thy increase in the third year, the year of the tithe, thou shalt give also unto the Levite, and unto the stranger, and unto the fatherless, and unto the widow; and they shall eat in thy villages, and be satisfied. And thou shalt say before the LORD thy God, I have brought forth the consecrated things out of my house, and have given them also unto the Levite, and unto the stranger, and unto the fatherless, and unto

the widow, according to all that thou hast commanded me: I have not transgressed thy commandments, neither have I forgotten them."

If Israel would keep His commandments, God promised to make them His people and place them in a special place among all the nations of the earth. And now we come to

Deuteronomy 27

———

Thus we come to one of the most fundamental sections of the book of Deuteronomy. This is the third speech of Moses. It belongs to the major section of the book that follows, which has to do with the future in the land. This is the third major section of the book, and extends from chapter 27 to chapter 30. It relates to the nation of Israel and the future of the promised land. In this section we find the so-called Palestinian covenant that God made with Israel.

We have called Deuteronomy chapters 28 through 30, the history of Israel in the Promised Land written before they entered the land. The section of Deuteronomy that comprises chapter 29 and extends to 30:10 is the Palestinian Covenant.

As we begin this new section, we will say a few words regarding a covenant. This word has already appeared several times. There are different kinds of covenants. We find that men make covenants with each other. Covenants of this nature are mentioned in the Bible. Then we have nations making covenants with each other and some of these are also mentioned in the Bible. Then we have the covenants that God made with His people and with all mankind, mentioned in the Old Testament. We have already studied the covenant made with Adam, the covenant made with Noah, the covenant made with Abraham and the covenant made with Moses. We are now in the part of the Bible that speaks of the Palestinian Covenant.

The covenants God makes are divided into two different classifications: conditional and unconditional. We could call them eternal covenants and provisional or temporary covenants. The everlasting covenant is a permanent covenant and is unconditional. The temporary covenant is a conditional covenant. It is important to distinguish between the two.

The covenant God made with Abraham was an unconditional covenant. The covenant God made with Moses, the Ten Commandments, was a conditional covenant. It says in Exodus 19:5: *"Now therefore, if ye will obey my voice, and keep my covenant, then ye shall be my peculiar treasure"* ... The Palestinian Covenant that we find in the chapters we are about to study, is an unconditional covenant.

This covenant has to do with the future of Israel. We have already seen that the Israelites were then on the eastern side of the Jordan River. They were preparing to enter the land. Now, this was the new generation. The old generation, as we have already seen, had died in the wilderness. Moses himself would not enter that land. We will see that this book ends with a prayer of blessing from Moses. He would die, but the people would enter the promised land under a new leader. Now, this particular section is prophetic and relates to the future of the Israelites in the land they were about to enter. We find here some of the most extraordinary prophecies in all of God's Word. Let us read verses 1 through 3 of this 27th chapter of Deuteronomy.

Moses and the elders of Israel commanded the people, saying, "You shall keep all the commandments which I command you this day. And in the day that you pass over Jordan into the land which the LORD your God is giving you, you shall set up large stones, and overlay them with lime; and you shall write on them all the words of this law, when you have passed over to go into the land which the LORD your God is giving you, a land flowing with milk and honey, as the LORD God of your fathers has spoken to you."

They were commanded that when they crossed the river, they should come to the Promised Land, and write the Ten Commandments on large stones that would be like monuments, set up in the sight of all to remind them of the law. Their possession of the land and their dwelling there would be determined by their obedience to God. That was a conditional covenant. But the land would be given to them without condition. God had given that land to Israel, and that was an unconditional covenant. God would bring Israel back to that land. And it is important that we see this. Let's continue reading verses 4 through 8 of this 27th chapter of Deuteronomy:

"When thou art come over Jordan, thou shalt set up these stones, which I command thee this day, in mount Ebal, and overlay them with lime; and thou shalt build there an altar unto the LORD thy God, an altar of stones; thou shalt not lift up upon them an instrument of iron. Of whole stones shalt thou build the altar of the LORD thy God, and shalt offer upon it a burnt offering unto the LORD thy God; and thou shalt sacrifice peace offerings, and eat there, and rejoice before the LORD thy God. And thou shalt write upon the stones very plainly all the words of this law."

God's law was to be placed in a prominent place. In fact, it was to be displayed before them wherever they went, even on the doors of their homes. They were to live in complete obedience to God. Let us now read verses 9 through 12:

"And Moses with the priests the Levites spake unto all Israel, saying, Keep silence, and hearken, O Israel: this day thou art become the people of the LORD thy God. Thou shalt therefore obey the voice of the LORD thy God, and do his commandments and his statutes, which I command thee this day. And Moses commanded the people on that day, saying, When thou art passed over Jordan, these shall stand upon mount Gerizim to bless the people: Simeon, Levi, Judah, Issachar, Joseph, and Benjamin."

When they entered the Promised Land, the blessing of the people was to be pronounced from Mount Gerizim. And Moses designated the tribes that would pronounce the blessing. Now let us read verse 13 of this 27th chapter of Deuteronomy:

> *"And these shall stand upon Mount Ebal to pronounce the curse: Reuben, Gad, Asher, Zebulun, Dan, and Naphtali."*

The tribes that were to pronounce the curses had to be on Mount Ebal. These mountains were located in the region where, according to the Gospel of John, the Samaritan woman would come to the well, in the time of Jesus' life. That well is still there. The blessings were therefore pronounced from Mount Gerizim and the curses from Mount Ebal.

Now, a list of the curses is presented. After entering the promised land, their possession of that land depended on one condition: We could compare them to tenants who had to pay rent. God was the owner of the land, and the rent would be obedience to God. However, they were more than tenants because God had given them that land as an eternal possession. Now, when a generation did not obey God, that generation would be expelled from the land, even though the land continued to be theirs as an eternal inheritance. That is why that portion of land, has been and is the most sensitive place in that part of the world. A list of twelve curses is now given and we will not go into details because they are self-explanatory. Let's just read a few verses. First of all verse 15 of this 27th chapter of Deuteronomy:

> *"Cursed be the man that maketh any graven image or molten image, an abomination unto the LORD, the work of the hands of the craftsman, and maketh it in secret. And all the people shall answer and say, Amen".*

This curse is related to the Ten Commandments, specifically to the first two. And verse 16 says:

> *"Cursed be he who dishonors his father or his mother. And all the people shall say: Amen".*

Here reference is made to the fifth of the Ten Commandments. Finally, let us read verse 26:

"Cursed be he that confirmeth not the words of this law to do them. And all the people shall say: Amen".

If you read all the verses in this chapter you will see that they all deal with the subject of breaking the Ten Commandments. And so we conclude our study of Deuteronomy chapter 27. We turn now to

Deuteronomy 28:1-15

———

This chapter continues to speak of Israel's future. Moses pronounced the conditional part of the covenant. The blessings in that land would be determined by the Israelites' obedience to God. Their disobedience would bring the curses, which are expressed here.

Then we have one of the most remarkable passages of Scripture, which presents in advance the history of this people in the land, even before they entered it. There are the prophecies of when they would be dispossessed of the land, which have been fulfilled in their entirety. And there are three prophecies of their restoration: two of them have already been fulfilled. And the third return of Israel to the land is yet future. Let us begin by reading the first two verses of this 28th chapter of Deuteronomy:

"And it shall come to pass, if thou wilt hearken diligently unto the voice of the LORD thy God, to keep and to do all his commandments which I command thee this day, that the LORD thy God shall also exalt thee above all the nations of the earth. And all these blessings shall come upon thee, and overtake thee, if thou shalt obey the voice of the LORD thy God".

This is a conditional part of the covenant. They would only be blessed if they obeyed God. Let us continue reading verses 3 through 6 of this chapter 28 of Deuteronomy:

"Blessed shalt thou be in the city, and blessed shalt thou be in the field. Blessed shall be the fruit of thy womb, and the fruit of thy ground, and the fruit of thy cattle, and the increase of thy herds, and the flocks of thy flocks. Blessed shall be your basket and your

kneading trough. Blessed shalt thou be when thou comest in, and blessed shalt thou be when thou goest out."

As you read this, you may be struck by the fact that twelve curses are pronounced, but there are only six blessings. Now, if you want to know why this is so, we will tell you when we get to the other blessings. In the New Testament we will see that our Lord stood on a mountain and delivered what we know as the Sermon on the Mount. Now, how did He begin that sermon? You will recall that in the gospel of Matthew 5:3, He said, *"Blessed are the poor in spirit, for theirs is the kingdom of heaven."* Then we have the other beatitudes that follow. Our Lord began His Sermon thus, in that way, because in that way He would capture the attention of the educated Israelite, who would hear about the blessings that would come to them after a prolonged history of ups and downs, sometimes favorable, sometimes adverse. They had already known captivity twice, and had been brought back to the promised land. But they were yet to experience another captivity that would disperse them all over the world.

There was the promise of a blessing if they obeyed him. Let us turn now to verses 13 and 14:

"The LORD shall make thee the head, and not the tail; and thou shalt be above only, and shalt not be beneath, if thou shalt obey the commandments of the LORD thy God, which I command thee this day, to keep and to do them, and if thou turn not aside from all the words which I command thee this day, to the right hand, or to the left, to go after other gods, to serve them."

Let us also read verse 15, to introduce us to the subject of that,

Disobedience would bring punishment

"But it shall come to pass, if thou wilt not obey the voice of the LORD thy God, to seek to do all his commandments and his statutes which I command thee this day, that all these curses shall come upon thee, and overtake thee."

Again we see that this was conditional, subject to the attitude of obedience they should adopt before God. As our time has come to an end, we will continue to consider this chapter 28 of Deuteronomy. And we will see the history of Israel in the Promised Land written in advance, before their entrance, that is, prophesied. We are left with only a brief reflection after having read so much about the obedience that God requires of human beings. He is the Creator and He knows that our own present and future good depends on a harmonious relationship with Him. And He has provided the way for human beings to come into His very presence by sending Jesus Christ to die for us. When a person accepts by faith that work of salvation, he initiates a relationship with God, receives forgiveness and eternal life and begins to enjoy a process of transformation and fellowship with the Creator. In this way, the transitory passage through this world, already enjoying the blessings that He sends upon His children, becomes a foretaste of the life that extends beyond this life, that is, eternal life.

Deuteronomy 28:32 - 29:29

———

W e continue our study of Deuteronomy chapter 28. And now we come to one of the most extraordinary passages of Scripture. It is the history of Israel in the Promised Land, written in advance, that is, prophesied. Scripture has three prophecies related to Israel or the Israelites, about their exile from the promised land and their return to be reunited in that land. There would be three banishments and three returns of Israel.

The first of these was prophesied by God to Abraham. You surely remember that in Genesis 15: 13 and 16, we read: *"Behold, thy seed shall dwell in a strange land, and shall be slaves there, and shall be oppressed four hundred years"* ... Then verse 16 says: *"And in the fourth generation they shall return hither"* ... In other words, they went to Egypt for 430 years, but then God brought them out of Egypt. That episode is the one we are following now in the book of Deuteronomy. The Israelites were then on the eastern side of the Jordan River and God was leading them back to the land in what would be their first return. In the book of Joshua we will find them entering the land, and in the book of Judges we will find them already established in the Promised Land, thus making this prophecy complete and literally fulfilled.

Now, the second time they were to be banished from the earth is mentioned here, and it is mentioned before they had even entered the earth. This is a very remarkable chapter. Let us read verses 32 through 37 of this 28th chapter of Deuteronomy:

"Thy sons and thy daughters shall be given to another people, and thine eyes shall see it, and shall faint for them all the day long; and there shall be no strength in thine hand. The fruit of thy land and of

175

all thy labor shall eat a people whom thou hast not known; and thou shalt be oppressed and broken all the days. And thou shalt be mad because of that which thou shalt see with thine eyes. The LORD shall smite thee with an evil boil upon thy knees and upon thy legs, from the sole of thy foot unto the crown of thy head, and thou shalt not be healed. The LORD shall bring thee, and the king whom thou hast set over thee, unto a nation which thou hast not known, neither thou nor thy fathers; and there shalt thou serve other gods, wood and stone. And thou shalt be a terror, and a reproach and a derision unto all people, whither the LORD shall bring thee.

This was to be the Babylonian captivity, which is now a fact in history. We will learn of this later in our study of the Bible, where we will read more prophecies concerning this in Jeremiah, and then actually see it happen. The historical record of the captivity is found in the books of Kings and Chronicles. The fact is that the army of the Chaldeans put out the eyes of the last king Zedekiah. His sons were slain before him, and then his eyes were put out. Thus we see how this literally fulfills verse 32. King Zedekiah was carried blind into Babylonian captivity.

Now, why did all this happen to them? It was because of their disobedience. God had given them the conditions. He had told them that if they obeyed, they would be blessed. But if they disobeyed, they would be punished.

Now, Israel returned from the Babylonian captivity. There was a return to the promised land. And we see this in the books of Ezra and Nehemiah. The prophets Haggai, Zechariah and Malachi, spoke of their return to the land. This, then, was the second prophecy that they would be banished from the land because of their disobedience, but they would return. That prophecy has been literally fulfilled.

The third dispersion of Israel would take place after they were conquered by Rome. This dispersion was described prophetically. Let us read verses 48 to 53 of Deuteronomy chapter 28:

"Therefore shalt thou serve thine enemies whom the LORD shall send against thee, in hunger, and in thirst, and in nakedness, and in want of all things; and he shall put a yoke of iron upon thy neck, until he have destroyed thee. The LORD will bring against thee a nation from far, from the uttermost part of the earth, that flieth as an eagle, a nation whose tongue thou canst not understand, a nation fierce in countenance, that will not regard an old man, nor spare a child; and will eat the fruit of thy cattle, and the fruit of thy land, until thou be destroyed; and will leave thee neither corn, nor new wine, nor oil, nor the increase of thy herd, nor the flocks of thy flock, until thou be destroyed. And he shall lay siege to all thy cities, until thy high and fortified walls, in which thou trustest, fall down in all thy land: therefore shall he lay siege to all thy cities, and to all the land which the LORD thy God hath given thee. And thou shalt eat the fruit of thy womb, the flesh of thy sons and of thy daughters, which the LORD thy God hath given thee, in the siege and in the distress wherewith thine enemy shall distress thee."

The historian Josephus, told of the coming of the Romans under Titus. Rome, known as the iron empire, fulfilled this prediction...Now, verse 48 of this 28th chapter of Deuteronomy says, *"And he shall put a yoke of iron upon thy neck."* The Romans came from the west. Their language was not an eastern language. The nation of Israel spoke a language that was related to the languages of Asia and Africa and the Orient, and it was totally different. God said they would not understand the language of the conquering nation. The eagle was the insignia of the Roman army, and God said that the invaders would fly like the eagle. We believe that many Israelites, who were educated, when they looked over the crenellated walls and saw the banners of Titus with the eagle insignia, must have said to themselves: "This is the fulfillment of the prophecy".

Josephus told us in his history that the mothers were forced to give up their babies, who were eaten. The Israelites died and their corpses were collected inside the city, and they had to be thrown out on the other side of the wall. this prophecy was literally fulfilled. And then, the Jewish people were scattered throughout the world. Let us turn now to verse 64:

> *"And the LORD will scatter you among all peoples, from one end of the earth to the other end of the earth; and there you shall serve other gods, which you and your fathers did not know, wood and stone."*

The Israelites have never returned from that dispersion. That part of the prophecy has not yet been fulfilled. There are three prophecies concerning the exiles. And there are three prophecies that speak of their return. They have returned twice, but they have not yet returned the third time.

So we have six prophecies in all, five of which have been literally fulfilled. Five of them have been literally fulfilled. How about the sixth one? We can tell you what we believe about it. We believe it will be literally fulfilled and will occur in the future. Let's read verses 65 through 67:

> *"And even among these nations thou shalt not rest, neither shall the sole of thy foot have rest: for there the LORD shall give thee a fearful heart, and faintness of eyes, and sorrow of soul; and thy life shall be as a thing hanging before thee, and thou shalt be afraid night and day, and shalt have no assurance of thy life. In the morning thou shalt say, Would that it were evening, and in the evening thou shalt*

say, Would that it were morning, for the fear of thine heart wherewith thou shalt be afraid, and for the sight of thine eyes.

How literally all this has been fulfilled through the persecutions of the Jews down through the centuries! All this is the consequence of their continual disobedience. Without rest, and with a fearful heart. In the morning wishing it were already evening, and in the evening wishing it were already day. What a sad situation that is! God is faithful to His Word, what a lesson there is for us!

This should impel us to share the gospel with those who have been banished from the Promised Land. The gospel of the Lord Jesus Christ is equally for the Jew as for the non-Jew. And it is as the apostle Paul says in Romans 1:5: *"that in all nations there may be those who believe in him and obey him".*

Deuteronomy 29:1-29

I n this chapter we have "the Palestinian Covenant". Chapters 29 and 30 of Deuteronomy are considered to be the Palestinian Covenant. Dr. Chafer considered chapters 28 to 30 as the Covenant. The Scofield Bible with References says that the Covenant begins in chapter 29 and goes through chapter 30:10, with chapter 29 as the introduction. In our notes we consider the Covenant beginning with chapter 29 and continuing through chapter 30:10. Although the Covenant proper is found in the first ten verses of chapter 30 and chapter 29 is preliminary.

Let us then look at the words of introduction to the Palestinian Covenant. This now, is the fourth speech of Moses. Let us read the first verse of this 29th chapter of Deuteronomy, which he goes on to give us,

A summary of God's care

"These are the words of the covenant which the LORD commanded Moses to make with the children of Israel in the land of Moab, besides the covenant which he made with them in Horeb."

T he covenant God made with them at Horeb consisted of the Ten Commandments. We know them as the Mosaic Law. The covenant that God was going to make with them here had to do with the land, and is called the Palestinian Covenant. God made this covenant with them shortly before they entered the land. Let us continue reading verse 2:

"And Moses called all Israel, and said unto them, Ye have seen all that the LORD hath done before your eyes in the land of Egypt unto Pharaoh, and unto all his servants, and unto all his land."

These Israelites were children and teenagers when they witnessed some of these incidents. The older people in the nation would have been in their sixties, after traveling through the wilderness. Only Joshua and Caleb remained from the older generation. Let us continue reading verses 3 and 4:

"the great trials which your eyes have seen, the signs and the great wonders. But unto this day the LORD hath not given you an heart to understand, nor eyes to see, nor ears to hear."

Despite seeing all these signs, they still did not perceive the scope of God's portentous intervention in their history. Isaiah said the same thing, and we see that the apostle Paul in Romans 11:8 made mention once again of Israel's blindness. Said the apostle Paul: *"As it is written, God hath given them an insensible spirit, eyes that they should not see, and ears that they should not hear, even unto this day"*.

Does this mean that God did not allow them to understand, that He closed their eyes and ears? No. It means that they already had them closed. Until God opens the eyes and ears of men and women, they cannot hear the gospel. Now, let this be clear, they can hear the Word of God, but they cannot hear the gospel with understanding.

It is necessary for the Spirit of God to work through the Word of God, to open the eyes and hearts of people, so that they see that the Word of God is effective and transforms the lives of human beings.

Now, God said that He simply left the Israelites in the same spiritual situation they were in. They had no intention of turning to Him. They had broken their relationship with the living and true God. And for that, and as punishment, God simply left them in their state of unbelief. Let us now read verse 5 of this 29th chapter of Deuteronomy:

> *"And I have brought you forty years in the wilderness; your garments have not waxed old upon you, neither have your shoes waxed old upon your foot."*

Imagine walking for forty years without your clothes and shoes wearing out. Now, Moses went on to describe his journey through the wilderness, and spoke of how these experiences must have opened his eyes.

There are many today who say that if God would only perform a miracle before their eyes, they would believe. Now these Israelites of Biblical history saw miracles for forty years and yet they did not believe. It is not for lack of evidence that men are unconverted or unbelieving. They are unbelievers not because of what they read in the Bible, nor because of what they see around them. The problem is within themselves. They are unbelievers because they are innate enemies of God, that is, by nature. They have no capacity to perceive the things of God.

What a picture God presents of the human heart! He says it is perverse. No one can truly conceive how terrible it really is. The apostle Paul said in Romans 8:7 and 8, *"Those who are concerned only with human things are enemies of God, because they are neither willing nor able to submit to his law. Therefore, those who live subject to the desires of the weak human condition cannot please God."* Now, Paul wrote these words after God tested Israel for 1500 years under the law. What a description of humanity this is! Those who live controlled by their human nature cannot please God.

Moses then gave them a summary of their history, reminding them of God's marvelous provision and care, and this was the preliminary to the covenant. Thus we arrive at a paragraph that we could title,

Blessings depended on obedience

Let us remember that the Palestinian covenant was unconditional, but that the possession of the land would depend on their obedience, Let us read verses 10 to 13:

"Ye all stand this day before the LORD your God, the heads of your tribes, your elders, and your officers, all the men of Israel, your little ones, your wives, and your strangers that dwell in the midst of your camp, from him that hews your wood to him that draws your water; That thou mayest enter into the covenant of the LORD thy God, and into his oath, which the LORD thy God maketh with thee this day, to establish thee this day for his people, and that he may be unto thee a God, as he hath said unto thee, and as he sware unto thy fathers Abraham, Isaac, and Jacob."

Let us now turn to consider,

The results of disobedience

When we read Moses' warnings that disobedience to the covenant would affect both the people and the land, it sounds to us like a prediction because the Israelites abandoned the covenant. Let us read verses 22 to 27:

"And the generations to come, your children that shall arise after you, and the stranger that shall come from far countries, shall say, when they shall see the plagues of that land, and the diseases thereof, whereof the LORD hath made it sick (brimstone and salt, all the land thereof being burned up); It shall not be sown, neither shall it bring forth, neither shall any herb grow therein, as in the destruction of Sodom and Gomorrah, Admah and Zeboiim, which the LORD destroyed in his anger and in his wrath): moreover all the nations shall say, Why hath the LORD done this unto this land?

184

Why hath the LORD done this unto this land? What meaneth the fierceness of this great wrath? And they shall answer: Because they forsook the covenant of the LORD God of their fathers, which he made with them when he brought them out of the land of Egypt, and went and served other gods, and bowed themselves unto them, gods which they knew not, and which they had not given them any thing. Therefore the anger of the LORD was kindled against this land, to bring upon it all the curses written in this book."

Dr. George Gill once told of a trip he had made by train going through Asia Minor to enter Palestine. He said that in the afternoon he had left Jerusalem and arrived in the Dead Sea region. As the train was leaving, he met on the rear platform a very wealthy American. The American said to him, "I have always heard that this was a land flowing with milk and honey. Well, I have never seen a land that is as bad as this." Dr. Gill said, "Do you know that it is interesting that you should say that? And he then proceeded to open his Bible, and looking up the pages of the book of Deuteronomy, he showed this tourist verse 22, here where it says that a foreigner would come from distant lands and ask that very question. The foreigners would ask the meaning of it all. They would ask why the land had changed so much. And Dr. Gill told him the precise reason, the one that Moses had given 3,500 years ago. He said, "Because they forsook the covenant of the Lord, the God of their fathers."

The land and the people were included together. In fact, the whole Mosaic system was adapted for that land. It was not only about the people, but also about the land. In the time of our Lord, the Mount of Olives was covered with trees. It was a wooded region. The enemies who came to conquer the country cut down the trees on the mountain and left the land desolate. God's judgment not only fell upon the people, but also upon the land. Let us turn now to verses 28 and 29 of this 29th chapter of Deuteronomy.

"And the LORD rooted them out of their land in anger, and in wrath, and in fury, and in great indignation, and cast them into another land, as it is seen this day. The secret things belong to the LORD our God; but those things which are revealed belong to us and to our children forever, that we may do all the words of this law".

But even before the covenant was made, the people were told what would happen in the end.

Now, there are many things that the Lord has not told us much about. But there are certain things that he has revealed to us. And for sure, he has told us about that land. It is desolate right now and they are trying to get water for it. The agricultural authorities have said that if the land could be rehabilitated by irrigation, it would be able to support 15 to 25 million people.

Anyone traveling in those lands today will surely wonder what this great judgment means in a land that was so rich in agriculture and livestock. The Israelites were expelled from that land because they did not keep the covenant, they did not fulfill the conditions established by God; they did not obey him. Now, does this mean that having failed to keep the covenant, the Israelites will never return to that land? Of course not. For God has made with them the Palestinian Covenant, which was unconditional. We will examine this in the next chapter.

And so we conclude our study of Deuteronomy chapter 29. We are left with a personal reflection. The prophecy fulfilled in history reinforces our confidence in the fulfillment of the prophecy that has not yet been fulfilled, because just as it happened in the past, God fulfills what he promises. Thus history confirms the authority of God's written Word. And since we are part of that history, we would do well to listen to that divine Word which is correct in its diagnosis of the ills of humanity, and of each one of us, providing the remedy found in Jesus Christ, the incarnate Word of God, who by his work on the cross saves us, begins to transform us, and gives us eternal life.

Deuteronomy 30:1-20

———

C ontinuing our study in the book of Deuteronomy, we come to chapter 30. In this chapter we find the Palestinian Covenant itself, which God made with Israel. You will notice that in this covenant there were no conditions. It began by saying what would happen and that they, that is, the Israelites, would turn to the Lord their God. God Himself would change their hearts. This was an unconditional promise of future blessing. Let us read the first three verses of this 30th chapter of Deuteronomy.

"And it shall come to pass, when all these things shall come upon thee, the blessing and the curse which I have set before thee, and thou shalt repent in the midst of all the nations whither the LORD thy God hath cast thee, and shalt turn unto the LORD thy God, And thou shalt obey his voice according to all that I command thee this day, thou and thy children, with all thy heart and with all thy soul; then the LORD shall bring again thy captives, and have mercy upon thee, and shall gather thee again from among all the people whither the LORD thy God hath scattered thee."

God made seven great promises here. He made these statements, which were unconditional. Verse 1 says that they would be scattered among all nations. The nation of Israel would be uprooted from their land because of their unfaithfulness. And that is what has happened.

Verse 2 says that there will be a future repentance of Israel in their dispersion; and that they will turn to God. Perhaps someone will ask if their return will be on the basis of their obedience. It seems logical that if they were scattered because of their disobedience, they will return because of their obedience. But, this is the order of grace and not the order of law. They will not return because they are obedient, but they will be obedient because of their return. God will bring them back to the land. The return of Israel to their own land is the subject of some twelve major prophecies in the Old Testament, and we will consider them carefully when we come to their corresponding study.

Now, verse 3 says that their Messiah will return. And pay close attention to this because it is very important. This phrase "he will return to gather you" ... in this verse, the return of the Lord Jesus Christ is implied. This is the first mention of Christ's return to earth. We could read it like this: *"Then the Lord will return to gather you from among all peoples"* ... The prophet Amos confirmed it when he spoke of this same matter in chapter 9 of his prophecy, verses 9 to 14, in particular verse 11 where he said: *"In that day I will raise up the fallen tabernacle of David, and will close up its breaches and raise up its ruins, and will build it as in the days of old"* ... The expression "In that day" ... in this verse, refers to the day of the return of the Lord Jesus Christ. And the Apostle James quoted these words, speaking in the 15th chapter of the book of the Acts of the Apostles, verses 15-17, when he said: "And with this agree the words of the prophets, as it is written, After this I will return and build again the tabernacle of David, which is fallen down, and will repair the ruins thereof, and will raise it up again, that the rest of men may seek the Lord, and all the Gentiles, upon whom my name is called". Now, when we come to the epistle of St. Jude, in the New Testament, we will see that Enoch mentioned the fact that Christ will return, but that prophecy was not included in the Old Testament. This is an extraordinary prophecy, but it has not yet been fulfilled. (There will be peace in that land at that time, as the prophet Jeremiah expresses it in chapter 23 of his prophecy, verses 1 to 8 and also in chapter 33, verses 6 to 18).

Turning now to Deuteronomy chapter 30, let us read verses 4 and 5:

"Even if thy outcasts be in the uttermost parts that are under heaven, from thence will the LORD thy God gather thee, and from thence will he take thee: and the LORD thy God will bring thee again unto the land which thy fathers inherited, and it shall be thine; and he will do thee good, and multiply thee above thy fathers."

We have here the fourth great promise of God. Israel is going to be restored to the land. This is an unconditional promise. No amount of dispersions can change the fact that in the future God will bring them back to their own land, as verse 4 declares.

The fifth promise is that there will be a national conversion. Let us read verse 6 of this 30th chapter of Deuteronomy.

"And the LORD thy God shall circumcise thine heart, and the heart of thy seed, that thou mayest love the LORD thy God with all thine heart and with all thy soul, that thou mayest live."

We find this same promise reaffirmed in the prophecies of Jeremiah and Hosea, and the apostle Paul expressed it in his epistle to the Romans.

The sixth promise mentioned here declares that Israel's enemies will be judged. Israel will return and then obey the voice of the Lord. That is the order of grace. And then their enemies will be judged. Let's continue reading verses 7 and 8.

"And the LORD thy God shall lay all these curses upon thine enemies, and upon thy haters that persecuted thee. And thou shalt return, and obey the voice of the LORD, and do all his commandments which I command thee this day."

Finally, the seventh wonderful promise is that Israel will then receive her full blessing. Let us read verses 9 and 10 of this 30th chapter of Deuteronomy.

"And the LORD thy God shall make thee to abound in all the work of thine hands, and in the fruit of thy body, and in the fruit of thy cattle, and in the fruit of thy ground, for good: for the LORD shall again rejoice over thee for good, as he rejoiced over thy fathers, when thou shalt obey the voice of the LORD thy God, to keep his commandments and his statutes written in this book of the law; when thou turn unto the LORD thy God with all thy heart and with all thy soul."

When will be the day of Israel's return to its land? Is it taking place right now? Well, we cannot be dogmatic about what we do not know. It is clearly stated that when they return to their land, it will be in an attitude of obedience to God. There will be no blessing for them in the land until they return in obedience, with the new heart that God will give them. This will take place at the time God brings them back to the land. The present return to Israel is not taking place in obedience to God. We believe that the definitive return of Israel to their land, according to the promise of the covenant, is still a future and unconditional fact, because it will be God Himself who will bring them back to their land.

Let us now look at the final admonition in this 30th chapter of Deuteronomy. Let us read verses 11 through 14.

"For this commandment which I command thee this day is not too hard for thee, neither is it far off. It is not in heaven, that thou shouldest say, Who shall go up for us into heaven, and bring it to us, and cause us to hear it, that we may do it? Nor is it on the other side of the sea, that thou shouldest say, Who shall pass over the sea for us, and bring it to us, and cause us to hear it, that we may do it? For the word is very near to you, in your mouth and in your heart, that you may perform it."

Israel could not plead as an excuse that they did not know God's commandment. God had communicated it to them, and they knew it.

We too have a responsibility, we who live in an age when it is possible for us to hear the Gospel message. you do not have to go to heaven to obtain salvation. You do not have to cross the ocean to find it. Let us tell you, salvation is very close to you. It is as close as your own telephone; as close as a preacher or some other Christian who can communicate the Word of God to you. And you have a responsibility to act on what you have heard. You are responsible. That's where your free will comes in, dear listener. My responsibility is to proclaim the Word of God. I try to get that Word into your ear, but I can only go so far. From then on, it is up to you to decide, dear listener. It is my privilege to bring you the Word of God today; but after hearing it, it is up to you to do something about what you have heard.

We would like to spend a little more time here on these verses. This passage here in Deuteronomy is really prophetic and speaks of a day when Israel will return to God with all their heart and soul, and God will make a new covenant with them. Jeremiah said the following, back in chapter 31 of his prophecy, verses 31 to 33: *"Behold, the days are coming, says the Lord, when I will make a new covenant with the house of Israel and with the house of Judah. Not like the covenant that I made with their fathers in the day that I took their hand to bring them out of the land of Egypt; for they made void my covenant, though I was a husband to them, saith the Lord. But this is the covenant that I will make with the house of Israel after those days, says the LORD: "I will put my law in their mind, and write it on their heart; and I will be their God, and they shall be my people."*

Moses was speaking about the future, and Jeremiah was also referring to the future. God had made a covenant with Israel. Now in human transactions a covenant is a promise; that is, an agreement or a contract.

All the covenants God made with Israel are eternal covenants, except the Mosaic covenant which is the Ten Commandments. That covenant was temporary and was to continue until the coming of the promised descendants. But the Abrahamic covenant is eternal, and so is the Palestinian covenant. The prophet Ezekiel said in chapter 16 of his prophecy, verse 60: *"But I will remember my covenant which I made with thee in the days of thy youth, and I will establish with thee an everlasting covenant".* That is what makes it true. It is a literal covenant, an everlasting covenant, a covenant that God made with Israel. God never promised us that land.

This is projected forward; to the future time when they will be in their land. There will be salvation there for them. Why? Because Christ is the one who will institute this new covenant that is yet in the future. The apostle Paul referred to this subject and quoted in chapter 10 of his epistle to the Romans, verses 4 to 10, these verses that we are studying here in Deuteronomy, chapter 30. *Thus Moses writes of the righteousness which is by the law, The man that doeth these things shall live by them.* But of the righteousness which is by faith he says thus: Say not in thine heart, Who shall ascend into heaven? (that is, to bring Christ down); or, Who shall descend into the bottomless pit? (that is, to bring Christ up from the dead). But what does it say? The word is near you, in your mouth and in your heart. This is the word of faith which we preach: if you confess with your mouth that Jesus is Lord, and believe in your heart that God raised him from the dead, you will be saved. For with the heart man believeth unto righteousness; but with the mouth confession is made unto salvation".

The apostle Paul did not give us a direct quotation of the verses in Deuteronomy, but he made an application of those verses. The fact that Paul had recourse to Moses was a remarkable example of skillful and careful exegesis, and the apostle elaborated on it. For this is an important part of Scripture.

Now notice that Paul did not say that Moses wrote this. It was the righteousness which is by faith that *"...saith thus"* ... as we saw in verse 6 of this passage we just read in chapter 10 of the epistle to the Romans. Paul was not substituting faith for law in his epistle to the Romans. Rather, he was teaching that righteousness by faith was attested to by the law and the prophets. In the same letter to the Romans, chapter 3, verse 21, the apostle said, *"But now, apart from the law, the righteousness of God has been manifested, being witnessed by the law and the prophets."*

Thus, the passage in Deuteronomy is prophetic. It speaks of a day when Israel will return to God with all their heart and soul, and God will make a new covenant with them. They will not need to go to heaven, nor beyond the sea. Why? Because Christ has come. It will not be necessary to go up to heaven to bring Christ down. He has already come! Nor will it be necessary to raise him from the dead. He has already been resurrected! Going back in time, we see that these Israelites had been under the law for 1,500 years. They knew it by heart and as ritual, but the law had not brought righteousness. Christ came just as the law had come. Christ was not someone who was very distant. Christ had come and had been among them. He died and rose again among them. This righteousness by faith was available to them just as it is available to all of us today, because it has been preached for centuries, and it has come down to us. It is that righteousness which is by faith that says that it is not necessary to ascend to heaven, nor descend into the abyss to find Christ. He is near, in your mouth and in your heart. The day will come when God's people, Israel, will see this. The righteousness which is by the law had not brought salvation. But the righteousness that is by faith does bring salvation.

Turning now to Deuteronomy chapter 30, which we are considering, let us read verses 15 and 16:

"See, I have set before you this day life and good, death and evil; for I command you this day to love the LORD your God, to walk in His ways, and to keep His commandments, His statutes and His judgments, that you may live and multiply, and the LORD your God may bless you in the land which you are entering to take possession of it."

The Israelites' occupation and possession of the promised land and their blessing in it would be determined by their obedience. Moses gave a historical review and said that they would be taken out of the land when they disobeyed. But God promised to bring them back. Ultimately, He will bring them back and they will never ever go out again. Why? Because they will obey Him? No! But because God will fulfill His covenant. He will bring them back to their land, and then they will obey Him.

And so it is with us, dear listener. God asks us to trust in the Lord Jesus Christ as our personal Savior; and after that, He speaks to us concerning obedience. He says, *"If ye love me, keep my commandments."* (First there must be love for the Savior. Then, if we say there is, God asks us to obey Him).

Let us now turn to the final verse of this 30th chapter of Deuteronomy where verse 20 says:

"Loving the LORD thy God, and obeying his voice, and following him: for he is life unto thee, and length of thy days; that thou mayest dwell in the land which the LORD sware unto thy fathers, to Abraham, to Isaac, and to Jacob, to give them."

We repeat that love and obedience constitute the great theme of Deuteronomy. If this matter was of such importance to the Israelites, how much more important is it to you and to me in this day of grace, when we have received so much more light, so much more knowledge!

Since we have been given so much more, our responsibility is even greater today. One of the things for which I pray, more fervently than for anything else, is that I may be kept close to Him. Today we need to be close to the Lord Jesus Christ. That is very important!

And so we end our study of this 30th chapter of Deuteronomy. In our next segment, God willing, we will enter into chapter 31 where we find the last counsel of Moses. We will thus come to the last section of the book of Deuteronomy, which is a song of Moses and comprises chapters 31 through 34. This last section of the book of Deuteronomy, begins with the fifth speech that Moses delivered to the children of Israel and which is found in this book. We are now approaching the end of Moses' life. Everything we have studied so far in the Old Testament has been written by Moses. And much of this material has been about Moses himself. He has been a key person from the time the Israelites left the land of Egypt. He was the leader of Israel for 40 years; and he has left us a record of the 120 years of his life. The Bible highlighted both his weaknesses and his dedication and love for God and his people. He was one of the most eloquent Biblical examples of how God transforms a person, gives him a purpose and motivation to live and strengthens him to carry out a mission impossible to accomplish with limited human resources.

Deuteronomy 31:1-32:6

Today we continue our study in the book of Deuteronomy.

Deuteronomy 31

In this chapter we find the last counsel of Moses. We have now reached the last section of the book of Deuteronomy. It is a song of Moses and extends from chapter 31 to chapter 34. This last section of Deuteronomy begins with the fifth speech of Moses found in this book, which he delivered to the children of Israel.

We come to the end of Moses' life. Everything we have studied so far in the Old Testament has been written by Moses. And much of this material has been about Moses himself. He was a key person from the time the Israelites left the land of Egypt. He was the leader of Israel for forty years. He has left us a record of the one hundred and twenty years of his life. And then we see that he was preparing to die. So let's read the first two verses of this 31st chapter of Deuteronomy, which begin a paragraph that we could title,

The last advice of Moses

"And Moses went and spake these words unto all Israel, and said unto them, This day I am an hundred and twenty years old; I can neither go out any more, nor come in: besides this the LORD hath said unto me, Thou shalt not go over this Jordan."

There are two statements here concerning Moses. The first, that he was growing old.

The second statement was that God had clearly told Moses that he would not pass over the Jordan. This was because of his disobedience, when he struck the rock instead of speaking to him. God clearly stated that a new leader would lead the Israelites across the Jordan into the

Promised Land, and Moses would no longer be the leader. Let us continue reading verse 3:

"The LORD thy God, he will pass over before thee; he will destroy these nations before thee, and thou shalt inherit them; Joshua shall be he that shall pass over before thee, as the LORD hath said."

Moses did not choose Joshua. It was God who chose him to succeed Moses. We doubt that Moses would have chosen Joshua, had he had the opportunity to choose. In fact, Caleb seemed to make a better impression than Joshua as a leader, and it would have been more natural for him to be the new leader. Or, after all, Moses was human, and wouldn't Moses be more willing to choose one of his own sons to succeed him? So did the Pharaohs in Egypt, and it would have been natural for Moses to do the same. But, no. God chose Joshua to lead the Israelites across the Jordan River. Moses, then, was no longer indispensable.

What a great lesson this is for us! It teaches us that none of us is indispensable to God's episode. God uses each person in his or her own time, but when that person's time or period of work is over, God's work always goes on. When the time comes to depart from this world, God raises up another. That is what happened in this episode we read about. Let's read now verse 6 of this chapter 31 of Deuteronomy...

"Be strong and of good courage; fear ye not, neither be afraid of them: for the LORD thy God is he that goeth with thee; he will not fail thee, nor forsake thee."

Moses encouraged the people not to fear the enemy peoples who were in that land. Let us note that he repeatedly encouraged this generation by commanding them to enter the land. He had gone through the experience of Kadesh-barnea. He had seen the old fearful generation return to the wilderness. So Moses again and again encouraged this new generation to continue their journey, assuring them that God would lead them into this land. Now verse 7 of this 31st chapter of Deuteronomy reads:

"And Moses called Joshua, and said unto him in the presence of all Israel, Be strong and of good courage: for thou shalt go in with this people unto the land which the LORD sware unto their fathers to give them, and thou shalt cause them to inherit it."

This was good. This was as it should be. Moses encouraged Joshua in the presence of all the people. By encouraging Joshua, he was also encouraging the people. Let's continue with verse 8:

"And the LORD goes before thee; he will be with thee, he will not fail thee, neither forsake thee; fear thou not, nor be dismayed."

This was the same lesson Isaiah had to learn. Chapter 6 of Isaiah's prophecy begins as follows: "In the year that King Uzziah died, I saw the Lord sitting upon a throne, high and lifted up. Poor Isaiah! Uzziah had been a good king. But now he was dead, and so Isaiah believed that things would go wrong. Another king would arise and the nation would be ruined, so to speak. But what did Isaiah find when he entered the temple? He realized that God was still sitting on the throne. The true King of Israel and Judah was still sitting on the throne. He was not dead, He was not even sick. And Isaiah had to learn that even though King Uzziah had died, God was still alive and was still leading His people. Let us now read verse 9:

"And Moses wrote this law, and gave it to the priests the sons of Levi, who bare the ark of the covenant of the LORD, and to all the elders of Israel."

You will recall that the book of Deuteronomy is the collection of Moses' speeches. There are eight speeches in all. They were first spoken, and then they were written down. But Moses was the author of this law.

This has been the most hard-fought of the attacks launched against the Bible. The hypothesis is that Deuteronomy was written later by a priest, and that Moses did not write it. At first critics declared that writing did not exist in Moses' time. But archaeology has discovered that writing existed long before Moses. It was also claimed that the Pentateuch was merely a historical document, compiled shortly before 400 BC. These and other critical theories have arisen because the predictions that had been made about the decline that Israel would experience after its entry into the promised land were so accurate that non-believers have preferred to believe that Deuteronomy was written as history rather than prophecy.

Even at this time when the Israelites were ready to enter the Promised Land, one would believe that God would not take them into that land, if there was a likelihood that they would fail. However, God told Moses here exactly what would happen. When they entered the land, they would turn their backs on God. God knows human nature. He knows your person and mine, dear listener. He knows that we would turn away from Him were it not that He keeps us close to Him.

Let us now turn to verse 14 and read to verse 17, and see how the Lord spoke to Moses:

"And the LORD said unto Moses, Behold, the day of thy death is at hand: call Joshua, and wait ye in the tabernacle of the congregation, that I may give him the charge. So Moses and Joshua went and waited in the tabernacle of the congregation. And the LORD appeared in the tabernacle in the pillar of cloud: and the pillar of cloud stood over the door of the tabernacle. And the LORD said unto Moses, Behold, thou shalt sleep with thy fathers, and this people shall rise up and play the harlot after the strange gods of the land whither they go to be in the midst of it; and they shall forsake me, and break my covenant which I have made with them; and mine

anger shall be kindled against them in that day; and I will forsake them, and hide my face from them, and they shall be consumed; and many evils and troubles shall come upon them, and they shall say in that day: Are not these evils come upon me because my God is not in the midst of me?"

Now, we know that there are those who believe that we are different today. Let us tell you that the Lord Jesus said the same thing about the church in the gospel according to Luke, chapter 18, verse 8. The Lord Jesus said: *"But when the Son of Man comes, will he find faith on the earth?* The way the question was formulated in the Greek language, implies a negative answer. And the answer is no, he will not find faith. Here in the New Testament the apostasy of the Church is predicted, just as God predicted the apostasy of Israel in the Old Testament.

Today, you and I live in times of apostasy. Christians who in the past preached nothing more and nothing less than the Word of God have abandoned the emphasis on the Word of God and have turned away from the faith. We have seen people who have seemed firm in the faith, abandon the teachings of the Word of God. And don't think that the same thing cannot happen to you dear listener! That is why we pray to God to keep us close to Him. Let us now turn to verse 19 and read up to verse 21 of this 31st chapter of Deuteronomy:

"Now therefore write you this song, and teach it to the children of Israel; put it in their mouths, that this song may be a witness to me against the children of Israel. For I will bring them into the land which I sware unto their fathers, which floweth with milk and honey; and they shall eat, and be satisfied, and wax fat; and they shall turn unto other gods, and serve them, and shall be wroth with me, and break my covenant. And when many evils and distresses shall come upon them, then shall this song answer in their face as a witness, for it shall be remembered by the mouth of their descendants; for I know

what they intend beforehand, before I bring them into the land
which I swore to give them."

Music is a very important element. Music has a great influence on all of us. Music says something, and it has to communicate a message that brings people closer to the Lord.

Now, the song of Moses proper, we find it in the next chapter, Deuteronomy chapter 32: Let us turn now to verse 24 in this chapter 31 that we are considering and read down to verse 26:

"And when Moses had made an end of writing the words of this law
in a book until it was finished, Moses commanded the Levites that
bare the ark of the covenant of the LORD, saying, Take this book of
the law, and set it beside the ark of the covenant of the LORD your
God, and let it be there for a witness against you."

Now, this book was not a book like the ones we have today. It was more like a scroll or it could have been a tablet of clay. However, in Moses' time they had scrolls and this law was probably written on a scroll.

Recall that we are in the section we have entitled "the song of Moses". He was coming to his final report to the nation. He called the tribes to gather to him, just as the elder Jacob, shortly before he died, had gathered his twelve sons around him. The twelve sons had then become the twelve tribes, and formed one great nation. And so it was that Moses called them together. Let us read then the closing verses of this 31st chapter of Deuteronomy, verses 27 to 30:

"For I know thy rebellion, and thy stiff neck: behold, while I am yet
alive with you this day, ye rebel against the LORD: how much more
after my death? Gather unto me all the elders of your tribes, and
your officers, and I will speak these words in their ears, and will call
heaven and earth to witness against them. For I know that after my
death ye shall surely corrupt yourselves, and turn aside from the way

which I have commanded you, and that evil shall come upon you in the latter days, because ye have done evil in the sight of the LORD, to provoke him to anger with the work of your hands. Then Moses spake in the ears of all the congregation of Israel the words of this song, until he had finished it.

Let us say that this statement that Moses made about 3500 years ago is still accurate, still true. It has been fulfilled in a very literal way. It is also true of the whole human family. For the human race, separated from God, is completely corrupted. All we have to do today is to look around us, to see that this is true.

And so we conclude our study of Deuteronomy chapter 31.

Deuteronomy 32:1-6

I n this chapter we find "The song of Moses". The song of Moses was, in many respects, a work that the nation had to learn. It was like their national anthem. It was a song that God gave them; every Israelite was to know it and teach it to his children.

We said earlier that the songs of a nation influence a nation, perhaps more than the laws do. Now this song of Moses was truly prophetic. And let us consider some important aspects. Let's read verse 1 of this 32nd chapter of Deuteronomy, to begin a paragraph that we have entitled,

An invitation to listen

"Hear, O heavens, and I will speak; And let the earth hear the words of my mouth."

T he first four verses of Moses' song constitute the introduction. God called the heavens and the earth to witness the conditions under which He was placing Israel in the promised land. Now, when God was about to banish Israel from that land as a judgment, the prophet Isaiah recorded the same call. The fact is that this is how the book of Isaiah begins. Chapter 1, verses 1 and 2 of Isaiah's prophecy begins, *"The vision of Isaiah the son of Amoz, which he saw concerning Judah and Jerusalem in the days of Uzziah, Jotham, Ahaz, and Hezekiah, kings of Judah. Hear, O heavens, and give ear, O earth; for the LORD speaks: I have brought up children, and made them great, but they have rebelled against me".*

When God placed Israel in the Promised Land, He called heaven and earth to be witnesses. When God prepared to expel them from that land some 700 years later, He again called heaven and earth to be witnesses. God was not doing this on the sly. It was not something he was doing covertly. He was justified in expelling them from the earth. Let us now read verse 2 of this 32nd chapter of Deuteronomy:

"It shall drip down like rain my teaching; It shall distil like dew my reasoning; Like drizzle upon the grass, And like drops upon the turf."

Such is the Word of God. The psalmist said in Psalm 72, verse 6: *"He shall come down like rain upon the mown grass; as the dew that showers upon the earth"*. A woman who lost her husband, whom she loved dearly, said she could now understand the meaning of that verse in the Psalms. She was the cut grass, but God had descended upon her through His Word, like a gentle rain. That is the way the Word of God should descend upon our lives.

There are some regions in our countries that are dry and arid during the summer because of the scarcity of rain. But when winter comes and the rain comes down, everything changes. It seems that the earth opens up to receive it. The rain washes and moistens the leaves of the trees; the trees become green, the plants come to life and flowers bloom. The whole panorama changes. That is the way the Word of God should descend upon our hearts and lives. Let us now continue with verse 3 of this 32nd chapter of Deuteronomy:

"For I will proclaim the name of the LORD. O magnify our God."

How little of our present literature exalts God, or has anything good to say concerning Him! It usually misuses His name, and that is if it mentions Him at all. Now, verse 4 of this 32nd chapter of Deuteronomy reads:

"He is the Rock, whose work is perfect, For all his ways are uprightness; A God of truth, and without any iniquity in him; He is just and righteous."

This is a song about the rock. The word rock is used about seven times in this song. The Lord Jesus Christ was called the Rock. Today Christ is the chief cornerstone of the building, as 1 Peter 2:6 says. *God is the Rock.* His work is perfect. This song, therefore, exalts God. And today we should also exalt Him. The next aspect that we find here in this song of Moses, is that,

The nation acted wickedly in the face of God's grace

Let us read verses 5 and 6 of this 32nd chapter of Deuteronomy:

"Corruption is not theirs; their children's is the stain, O crooked and perverse generation: so do ye repay the LORD, O foolish and ignorant people? is he not your father that created you? he made you and established you."

God was the Father of the Israelites because He had created them. We also see that there is no mention of redemption here. In a sense God is the Father of all mankind because He created all mankind. When God created Adam, he was called the son of God, but Adam sinned. And after that, none of Adam's descendants were called children of God, unless they had become children of God through faith in Christ Jesus. As it says here, the whole human family can be described as a wicked and perverse generation, a foolish and unwise people.

And since a few moments ago we were talking about rain, a phenomenon as natural as it is necessary for the earth and human survival, we think it appropriate to end by recalling those words of the prophet Isaiah 55:10 and 11: "For as the rain and the snow come down from heaven, and return not thither, but water the earth, and make it bring forth and bud, and give seed to him that soweth, and bread to him that eateth; so shall my word be that goeth forth out of my mouth: it shall not return unto me void, but it shall accomplish that which I please, and it shall prosper in the thing whereto I sent it."

There are lives that are like dry, arid land. If that is your case, we invite you to be willing to receive the Word of God, which like the rain that descends from heaven, soaks the barren land and makes it produce fruit, can descend today upon your soul and where there was no spiritual life, He can create life, eternal life. And so, like that disciple named Peter, who would later be transformed by the risen Christ, he will be able to say: "Lord, to whom shall I go? You have the words of eternal life.

Deuteronomy 32:7 - 34:8

―――

Today we continue our study of Deuteronomy chapter 32. And we continue to consider the "Song of Moses". We have already seen two main aspects of this song. First, the "call to listen". Second, the "payment of evil" that the nation of Israel gave to God in response to His grace. We will begin today by reading verses 7 to 10, of this 32nd chapter of Deuteronomy, to consider the third aspect, namely,

The goodness of the Lord

"Remember the days of old, Consider the years of many generations; Ask thy father, and he will tell thee; Ask thy elders, and they will tell thee. When the most High made the nations to inherit, When he divided the children of men, He set the bounds of the people according to the number of the children of Israel. For the LORD'S portion is his people; Jacob is his inheritance which is his inheritance. He found him in a desert land, and in a wilderness of horrible solitude: he brought him round about, he instructed him, he kept him as the apple of his eye.

We have here something very interesting. This explains why even today, that land and the people in that land are a sensitive place in the world. Why? Because in the division of the earth, that land was reserved by the wisdom and goodness of God for the possession of His people and for the manifestation of His most extraordinary works. The scene was small, but admirably adapted for the observation of the human race, being the point of junction of the two great continents of Asia and Africa, and almost within the range of view of Europe. From that point as from a common center, the report of the wonderful works of God, the good news of salvation by the obedience and sufferings of

His Son Jesus Christ, could quickly and easily be carried to all parts of the earth. For that was God's purpose. And verse 10 reminds us that for 40 years in that great wilderness, God led His people and protected them. Why? Because they were like the apple of His eye. And this is a really endearing expression. And we come now to one of the great statements of Scripture. Let us now read verses 11 and 12 of this 32nd chapter of Deuteronomy:

"As the eagle that stirreth up her brood, Fluttering over her young, Spreading her wings, she taketh them, She beareth them on her feathers, Jehovah alone guided him, And with him there was no strange god."

When the little eaglets are developing their wings, they stay in the nest and their parents bring them food during the day, and then protect them during the night. But at last the day comes when the eagle pushes the eaglets off the high cliff where the nest is located and teaches them to fly. When one of them spreads its wings and struggles to fly, and doesn't do well, the mother reaches underneath with her huge strong wings and carries it back to the nest to continue feeding it for a few days, until it tries to fly again. God said that is what He does with His own. Sometimes He pushes us out of the nest, not because He does not love us, but because He wants us to learn to fly, that is, to live for Him. This is a wonderful description of the goodness of the Lord. Let us now read verse 15, to begin to see the fourth aspect that we find in this song of Moses, and that is,

The apostasy of the nation

"But Jeshurun waxed fat, and kicked (You grew fat, you covered yourself with fatness); Then he forsook the God who made him, And despised the Rock of his salvation."

Jeshurun was another name for Israel. Israel grew fat and kicked. Israel became affluent and the Israelites became complainers. In their prosperity, they no longer considered the Rock that delivered and sustained them to be important. And we, as Christians, living in an affluent society, are like them. And, unfortunately, we too complain. Now, let us read verses 16 to 18:

"They stirred him up to jealousy with strange gods: they provoked him to anger with abominations. They sacrificed to demons, and not to God; To gods whom they had not known, To new gods that came from near, Which your fathers had not feared. Thou hast forgotten the Rock that created thee; Thou hast forgotten God thy creator."

They forgot God, the one who saved and protected them, and fell into idolatry. This was the apostasy. Let us read verses 19 and 20 of Deuteronomy chapter 32, which describe it,

God's judgment on them

"And the LORD saw it, and was wroth with anger Because of the contempt of their sons and their daughters. And he said, I will hide my face from them, I will see what their end shall be: for they are a perverse generation, unfaithful children."

In this new section, which covers verses 19 to 25, we see the judgment that God sent upon His people. God said He would hide His face from them. (I wonder: Isn't the same thing happening today? We have heard from many Christians who have prayed for God to work in the world today, but He does not seem to work. Perhaps He hides His face from our nations). Sixth, let us read verses 26 and 27 of this 32nd chapter of Deuteronomy, from which we find another section entitled,

God's longing for his people

"I had said that I would scatter them far away, That I would cause the remembrance of them to cease from among men, That I had not feared the provocation of the enemy, Lest their adversaries should be puffed up, Lest they should say, Our mighty hand hath done all this, and not the LORD."

The section from verses 26 to 42, expresses this longing of God. He said that He would scatter Israel to distant lands, except that He feared that they would suffer the wrath of the enemy. He did not want their enemies to hurt or destroy them. For then the enemies would mock, boasting that they had succeeded in overcoming them by their power. Let us continue with verses 28 through 31:

"For they are a nation void of counsel, And there is no understanding in them: would that they were wise, that they might understand this, And realize the end that awaits them! How could one chase a thousand, And two put ten thousand to flight, If their Rock had not sold them, And the LORD had not delivered them up? For their rock is not as our Rock, And even our enemies are judges of it."

What a picture we have here! God had a longing for His people. He wanted to redeem them. He wanted to save them. And the last aspect that we find here in this Song of Moses, in verses 43 to 45, which we will read next, could be entitled,

The nations of the world blessed with Israel

"Praise his people, O ye nations, for he will avenge the blood of his servants, And take vengeance on his enemies, And make atonement for the land of his people. And Moses came and recited all the words

*of this song in the ears of the people, he and Joshua the son of Nun.
And Moses finished reciting all these words to all Israel."*

T hus we come to the last stanza of this song of Moses. The nations
of the world will be blessed with Israel. And it is very important
that we see this. Let us next read verses 46 and 47 of this 32nd chapter
of Deuteronomy. In which we can see,

Moses' final exhortation

*"And he said unto them, Apply your hearts unto all the words which I
testify unto you this day, that ye may command your children, that
they may observe to do all the words of this law. For it is not a vain
thing for you; it is your life, and by this law ye shall prolong your
days in the land whither ye go over Jordan, to possess it".*

A gain we can hear that possession of the land would depend on
their obedience. Israel was placed under the law and was to obey
it. It was through obedience that they would receive the blessing in that
land. And now let us read the last verses of this 32nd chapter of
Deuteronomy, verses 48 to 52:

*"And the LORD spake unto Moses the same day, saying: Go up into
this mount Abarim, into mount Nebo, which is in the land of Moab,
which is over against Jericho, and see the land of Canaan, which I
give for an inheritance unto the children of Israel; and die in the
mount whither thou goest up, and be joined unto thy people, as
Aaron thy brother died in mount Hor, and was joined unto his
people; Because ye sinned against me in the midst of the children of
Israel at the waters of Meribah of Kadesh in the wilderness of Zin;
because ye sanctified me not in the midst of the children of Israel.
Therefore you shall see the land before you, but you shall not go in
there, to the land which I give to the children of Israel".*

Moses, the representative of the law, the lawgiver, the lawgiver, could not enter the promised land. Legalism was really a hindrance. The law is a revealing element of sin. It can never take away sin. The law cannot save. In the course of this history we have proven that the law could not get Moses into the promised land. The law cannot bring us into the place of blessing.

And with this, we conclude our study of Deuteronomy chapter 32.

Deuteronomy 33

In this chapter we have the "Blessing of the Tribes". Moses gathered the people around him, by tribes, and blessed each one of them. We will not talk about each of the blessings in particular, but we will mention some details. Let us read the first verse of this 33rd chapter of Deuteronomy:

"This is the blessing with which Moses the man of God blessed the children of Israel before he died."

And it began with Reuben. It says in verse 6 of Deuteronomy chapter 33:

"Let Reuben live, and not die; And let not his men be few."

Moses prayed that the tribe of Reuben would never become extinct in Israel. Now verse 7 says:

"And this blessing he uttered for Judah. He said thus: Hear, O LORD, the voice of Judah, And bring him to his people; His hands shall be sufficient for him, And thou shalt be his help against his enemies."

Judah was the tribe of royalty, from which the Messiah would come, according to Jacob's prophetic blessing. Now, Moses prayed that Judah might accomplish the task of conquering the enemies. Let us now read verses 8, 10 and 11 of this 33rd chapter of Deuteronomy:

"To Levi he said, Thy Thummim and thy Urim shall be for thy godly man, whom thou hast proved in Massah, with whom thou hast contended at the waters of Meribah...They shall teach thy judgments unto Jacob, and thy law unto Israel: they shall lay incense before

thee, and burnt offerings upon thine altar. Bless, O LORD, what
they do, And receive with favor the work of their hands: Smite the
loins of their enemies, And of them that hate them, that they may
not rise up.

This tribe received the honor of constituting the priesthood in Aaron's family. It had the privilege of teaching the law. The nation would be blessed through the tribe of Levi.

According to verses 13 to 17, the blessing was to come to Israel through the tribe of Joseph. Actually, the tribe of Joseph included two tribes: the tribes of Ephraim and Manasseh. Now let's look at an interesting blessing found here in verse 24 of this 33rd chapter of Deuteronomy. Let's read it:

"To Asher he said, Blessed above the sons be Asher; Let him be the
beloved of his brethren, And dip his foot in oil."

The territory of Asher was famous for its olive trees, which grew in great profusion. Interestingly, years ago an oil pipeline entered the northern part of the kingdom, through the land of Asher. It may be that this pipeline will be used again. Let us now read verses 26 to 29 of this chapter 33 of Deuteronomy:

"There is none like the God of Jeshurun, Who rides upon the heavens
for thy help, And upon the clouds with his greatness. The everlasting
God is thy refuge, And here below the everlasting arms: He hath cast
out the enemy from before thee, And hath said, Destroy. And Israel
shall dwell in safety, the fountain of Jacob shall dwell alone In a land
of corn and wine: his heavens also shall drop down dew. Blessed art
thou, O Israel: who is like thee, O people saved by the LORD, the
shield of thy help, and the sword of thy triumph? So shall thine
enemies be humbled, and thou shalt tread upon their high places.

As we read these words, we can only exclaim: Ah, if only Israel had obeyed God! And so we conclude our study of Deuteronomy chapter 33.

Deuteronomy 34

I n this chapter we have the lonely and strange death of Moses. Perhaps the question arises as to whether Moses wrote about his own death. Well, he might well have done so. The Lord had already told him that he was going to die. However, many believe that this section here was part of the book of Joshua. And it may well have been, since originally there were not the divisions of books that we have today. In the beginning, the Old Testament was written in scrolls, and one book followed another without major interruption. Therefore, it may well be that this section we have here is the beginning of the book of Joshua. Let us read then, verses 1 to 6 of this chapter 34 of Deuteronomy:

"And Moses went up out of the plains of Moab unto mount Nebo, to the top of Pisgah, which is over against Jericho; and the LORD showed him all the land of Gilead unto Dan, and all Naphtali, and the land of Ephraim and Manasseh, and all the land of Judah unto the west sea, and the south, and the plain, and the valley of Jericho, the city of palm trees, unto Zoar. And the LORD said unto him, This is the land which I sware unto Abraham, unto Isaac, and unto Jacob, saying, Unto thy seed will I give it. I have permitted thee to see it with thine eyes, but thou shalt not pass thither. And Moses the servant of the LORD died there in the land of Moab, according to the word of the LORD. And he buried him in the valley in the land of Moab, over against Bethpeor; and no man knoweth the place of his sepulcher unto this day."

Moses could not enter the promised land. Now, why was the burial place of Moses kept secret? We learn from reading the universal epistle of St. Jude, verse 9, that the devil was wrestling with the Archangel Michael, disputing with him over the body of Moses. Satan did not want Moses to appear on the Mount of Transfiguration. But God was going to bring Moses to earth, through the Lord Jesus Christ. So God Himself took care of Moses' burial and entombment. And so Moses would be raised from the dead, brought to the earth and appear there with the Lord Jesus Christ. When Christ was transfigured on a mountaintop, Moses and Elijah appeared with Him on the Mount of Transfiguration, and talked about the approaching death of Jesus in Jerusalem. (We can read the account of that appearance in Matthew 17, in Mark 9 and Luke 9). So, in the end, Moses did eventually enter the Promised Land. The law could not bring him into the land; but the Lord Jesus Christ did. Let us read verses 7 through 9 of this 34th chapter of Deuteronomy, with which this book ends.

"Moses was an hundred and twenty years old when he died; his eyes were not dimmed, neither did he lose his strength. And the children of Israel mourned for Moses in the plains of Moab thirty days; and so the days of mourning and mourning for Moses were fulfilled. And Joshua the son of Nun was filled with the spirit of wisdom, because Moses had laid his hands upon him; and the children of Israel obeyed him, and did as the LORD commanded Moses."

It is with a note of sadness that this book of Deuteronomy concludes. However, there would also be rejoicing. Israel then stopped at the entrance to the Promised Land. They would enter it under the leadership of Joshua. And we will enter with them, as we study in our next segment, the book of Joshua. Let's read, finally, verses 10 through 12, the last verses of this book:

"And there arose no prophet in Israel like Moses, whom the LORD knew face to face; none like him in all the signs and wonders which the LORD sent him to do in the land of Egypt, to Pharaoh and to all his servants and to all his land, and in the great power and in the mighty and terrible acts which Moses did in the sight of all Israel."

Any prophet that may have arisen before this statement was not equal to Moses, nor was there after him until the coming of the One of whom Moses prophesied in 18:15, pointing to the future Messiah. As a prophet, Moses led the people after the deliverance from Egypt, delivered to them the revelation entrusted to him, and led them through the wilderness to the vicinity of the Promised Land. According to Exodus 33:11, Moses was the man who spoke with God face to face, as one who spoke with a friend, with a companion. And it was not only in word that God worked through Moses, but in deeds that would never be forgotten. The signs and wonders performed in Egypt constituted an element of the utmost importance in the development of the history of salvation, and pointed directly to the most significant of all acts of liberation in the history of mankind. We refer to the work of redemption accomplished by Jesus Christ on the cross and His resurrection from the dead. We would like to bid farewell today with an invitation from the poet Mariano San Leon, which we echo. In fact, the invitation is inspired by the Bible, by the Gospel. It is an old song that goes as follows:

Come to the cross, you who seek forgiveness. You may find peace, health, and eternal redemption. Come to the everlasting covenant of love, hear the voice of your Savior. How bitter your thirst, how far from virtue! You are no longer ignorant of the subtle net of your slavery. Come, the Cross of Christ is a spring of redemption and everlasting joy.

Conclusion

———

The book of Deuteronomy invites us to reflect on God's faithfulness and unconditional love for His people. Throughout its pages, we find fundamental teachings on the importance of obeying God's commandments, trusting in His provision and living a life consecrated to Him.

Let us remember that, like the people of Israel in Moses' time, we too are called to follow God with our whole being, to love and obey Him at all times. In the book of Deuteronomy, we see God's desire to bless His people when they walk in His will, but also the warning of the consequences of turning away from Him.

May each young person in our Bible class carry the lessons of Deuteronomy with them in their hearts, remembering that God is faithful and that we can rely on His guidance and care at all times. May we live lives that reflect His love, bringing His light to a world in need of hope and redemption.

At the end of our study in the book of Deuteronomy, let us remember that God is with us at every moment, strengthening us, guiding us and filling us with His grace and mercy. May we be courageous young people committed to the Lord, willing to follow His way and live according to His will. May the Word of God be our light and our guide at all times. May the blessing of the Lord be upon each one of you, young people of the Bible class! Amen!

Don't miss out!

Visit the website below and you can sign up to receive emails whenever Bible Sermons publishes a new book. There's no charge and no obligation.

https://books2read.com/r/B-A-MZBS-NHGDF

BOOKS 2 READ

Connecting independent readers to independent writers.

Did you love *Bible Class for Youth and Adults: Beginner's Guide: Deuteronomy*? Then you should read *Prophetic Profile: The Last Week, The Great Tribulation*[1] by Bible Sermons!

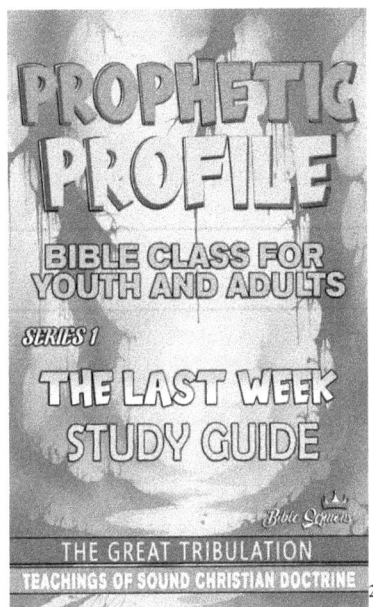

Join us through the pages of this book of biblical prophecy, where the mysteries of the last week and the great tribulation are unveiled. With a deep and revealing approach, each chapter will lead you to reflect on the events that will mark the end times, offering a unique perspective that will resonate in your heart and mind.

This series is not only a guide to what is to come, but also an invitation to prepare yourself spiritually for the challenges ahead. As you explore its teachings, *you will feel the urgency to understand and act, finding hope and strength in the midst of adversity.*

---

1. https://books2read.com/u/b56PPk

2. https://books2read.com/u/b56PPk

Also by Bible Sermons

A Collection of Biblical Sermons
The Power of Great Gospel Words
The Power of Prayer: Men Ought Always to Pray
The Power of the Single Life in Christ
Analyzing The Power of a Life in Christ

Bible Characters Collection
Analyzing Biblical Scenes: 62 Inspiring Christian Teachings from the
Old Testament

BIBLE CLASS FROM SCRATCH
Bible Class for Youth and Adults: Beginner's Guide: Genesis
Bible Class for Youth and Adults: Beginner's Guide: Exodus
Bible Class for Youth and Adults: Beginner's Guide: Leviticus
Bible Class for Youth and Adults: Beginner's Guide: Numbers
Bible Class for Youth and Adults: Beginner's Guide: Deuteronomy
Bible Class for Youth and Adults: Beginner's Guide: Introduction

Notes in the New Testament

Analyzing Notes in the Book of Matthew: Fulfillments of Old Testament Prophecies

Analyzing Notes in the Book of Mark: Finding Peace in Difficult Times

Analyzing Notes in the Book of Luke: The Divine Love of Jesus Revealed

Analyzing Notes in the Book of John: John's Contribution to the New Testament Scriptures

Analyzing Notes in the Book of the Acts of the Apostles: A Journey of Continuation in the Work of Jesus

Overflying The Bible

Symbols in the Bible: Healthy Christian Doctrine

Bible Introduction: Overflying The Bible from Genesis by Brethren in the Faith

Chronological Prophecy: Things That Will Happen on Earth

Bible Study: Genesis 1. Creation in Six Days

PROPHETIC PROFILE

Prophetic Profile: The Last Week, The Great Tribulation

Teaching in the Bible class

Sunday School Lessons: 182 Bible Stories

Bible Class for Beginners: 50 Beautiful Lessons

Lessons for Sunday School: 62 Biblical Characters

How to Teach in Sunday School: A Guide for Bible Class Teachers

Teaching in the Bible Classroom
Studying Teaching in the Bible Classroom: A Teacher's Guide

The Education of Labor in the Bible
Analyzing the Education of Labor in Genesis: The Purpose of Life on Earth
Analyzing the Teaching of Labor in Exodus: From Slavery to Liberation
Analyzing the Labor Education in Leviticus: The Spirit of the Law at Work
Analyzing the Labor Education in Numbers: Israel's Desert Experience for Today's Challenges
Analyzing the Labor Education in Deuteronomy: A Perspective on Working Life Today
Analyzing Labor Education in Joshua and Judges: Motivation for Hard work!
Analyzing Labor Education in Ruth: A Reference for Self-growth and Self-improvement
Analyzing Labor Education in Samuel, kings and Chronicles: A Study of Leadership in Antiquity
Analyzing Labor Education in Ezra, Nehemiah, Esther: A Look at the Past to Orient our Future Work
Analyzing Labor Education in Job: Spiritual and Professional Example for Working Life
Analyzing Labor Education in Psalms: Ethics, Works and Words
Analyzing Labor Education in Proverbs
Analyzing Labor Education in Ecclesiastes: "Hard Work Under the Sun," The Lessons of Ecclesiastes

God's Guide for Work: Discovering God's Will for a Particular Job
Analyzing Labor Education in Poetic Books
Analyzing Labor Education in the Prophetic Books of the Bible
Analyzing Labor Education in the 12 Prophets of the Bible
Analyzing Labor Education in the Old Testament

Standalone
Analyzing Notes in the 4 Gospels: Commentary Biblical
Analyzing What is to Come: God's Prophecies
The Prophetic Book Abdias: The Destruction of Edom

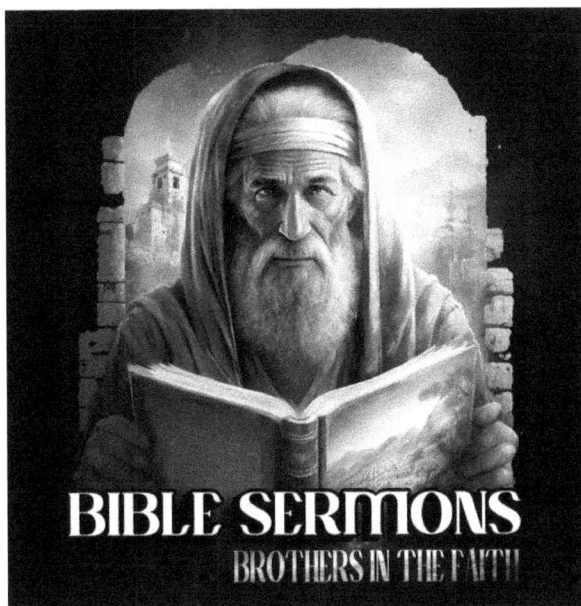

About the Author

This bible study series is perfect for Christians of any level, from children to youth to adults. It provides an engaging and interactive way to learn the Bible, with activities and discussion topics that will help deepen your understanding of scripture and strengthen your faith. Whether you're a beginner or an experienced Christian, this series will help you grow in your knowledge of the Bible and strengthen your relationship with God. Led by brothers with exemplary testimonies and extensive knowledge of scripture, who congregate in the name of the Lord Jesus Christ throughout the world.

Milton Keynes UK
Ingram Content Group UK Ltd.
UKHW021921281024
450365UK00017B/891

9 798227 914262